FAWLTY TOWERS

U.K. £2.5

Australia $7.

New Zealand $7.6

FAWLTY TOWERS

by John Cleese & Connie Booth

Ⓒ Contact Publications Limited

From the highly acclaimed BBC television series *Fawlty Towers*

Designed by John Rushton for
Contact Publications Limited
11 St John's Hill, London SW11

ISBN 0 8600 7598 2

Printed in Great Britain by Redwood Burn Limited,
Trowbridge and Esher

CONTENTS

THE BUILDERS

CAST

Basil Fawlty	**John Cleese**
Sybil Fawlty	**Prunella Scales**
Manuel	**Andrew Sachs**
Polly	**Connie Booth**
Major Gowen	**Ballard Berkeley**
Miss Tibbs	**Gilly Flower**
Miss Gatsby	**Renee Roberts**
O'Reilly	**David Kelly**
Lurphy	**Michael Cronin**
Jones	**Michael Halsey**
Kerr	**Barney Dorman**
Stubbs	**James Appleby**
Delivery Man	**George Lee**

In the lobby

Polly is behind the reception desk looking through some papers. She yawns. The phone rings.

Polly Hallo, Fawlty Towers . . . yes . . . yes, this afternoon, that'd be fine . . . no, it's <u>sixteen</u>, Elwood Avenue . . . yes, sixteen. Thank you.

Polly rings off. Basil comes down the stairs carrying a couple of suitcases. Sybil is behind.

Basil I'll just put these outside.

He goes out through the main entrance. Sybil comes over to Polly, and puts a sheet of paper on the desk beside her.

Sybil Polly, this is where we'll be if you need us. There's the number. So if Mr. Stubbs wants to know anything when he comes, just call, but <u>don't</u> if you don't <u>have</u> to, love, it's the first week-end we've had off since Audrey had her hysterectomy.

Polly Not to worry, I know what they've got to do. Oh, and somebody called about a garden gnome.

Sybil Oh, yes.

Polly It's in, and they're going to deliver it this afternoon.

Sybil Good.

Sybil looks around thoughtfully.

Sybil (*to herself*) Golf shoes.

Major Gowen crosses the lobby. Sybil sees him.

Sybil Good morning, Major.

Major Very well, thank you.

Sybil turns briskly back to Polly.

Sybil Now, does everyone know about dinner tonight?

Polly I think so.

Sybil But you'll be able to manage breakfast tomorrow, will you?

Polly Oh yes, there's only the Major and the ladies.

Sybil nods approvingly.

Sybil Now where are those shoes?

She makes for the drawing room. Polly yawns. Manuel enters from the dining room, talking to himself determinedly.

Manuel One moment please, I will het your vill. I will . . . hhhet your vill.

Polly Manuel.

Manuel stops.

Polly Get your bill.

Manuel Het your bill?

Polly Get, guh, guh.

Manuel Get! Guh, guh, guh! Ah!

Polly That's it.

Manuel nods enthusiastically and trots off.

Manuel I will get your vill.

*Sybil comes out of the drawing room with
her golf shoes. She sees Manuel.*

Sybil Oh, Manuel. Put these with the cases please. Polly!

*She gives the shoes to Manuel and goes
into the inner office. Polly goes after her.
Manuel looks at the shoes, and then around
the lobby, confused. Basil comes back in
through the main entrance.*

Basil Ah, Manuel! While we're . . .

Manuel spins round.

Manuel One moment please, I will get your bill!

He bows.

Basil . . . What?

Manuel I will get your bill. Si?

Basil What are you talking about?

Manuel Listen! Today . . . we have veef, beal or sothahhhes!

Basil What?!

Manuel Bang . . . hhhers.

Basil . . . Shut up.

Manuel Que?

Basil Shut up.

Manuel Ah! Si, si. 'Shut up.' Yes, I understand, yes.

Basil Well, will you shut up then?

Manuel (*keenly*) Si, si, shut up.

He nods excitedly.

Basil (*very slowly*) . . . While we're <u>away</u> . . . <u>gone</u> . . . <u>clean</u> all the <u>windows</u>.

Manuel nods blankly. A pause. Basil controls himself.

Basil Ooh! Quando nosotros somos . . . . . . what's 'away' in Spanish?

Manuel Que?

Basil 'Away.'

A pause.

Basil You <u>know</u> . . . '<u>away</u>'!

Manuel leaves.

Basil No, not <u>you</u>! <u>Us</u>!

He catches him.

Basil Clean the <u>windows</u>!!! (*Manuel stares. Basil points to the dining room*)

Manuel Green?

Basil <u>Clean</u>! . . . Look!

He takes a handkerchief out of his pocket, mimes, puts it in Manuel's hand and circulates the latter.

Manuel continues to circulate his hand uncomprehendingly.

Manuel Clean ?

Basil sighs and picks him up.

Basil Go on, go on ! !

Manuel rotates the handkerchief.

In the dining room

Major Morning Fawlty.

Basil Morning Major.

Basil Clean the windows!

Manuel continues to do so. Basil turns to leave but Miss Tibbs and Miss Gatsby have blocked his exit. They look playful.

Miss Tibbs Mr. Fawlty.

Basil Ah, good morning. Good morning, ladies.

Miss Tibbs Ursula and I think you're a very naughty boy, don't we, Ursula?

Miss Gatsby winks knowingly. Basil's smile narrows, but he widens it again expertly.

Basil Oh really?

Miss Tibbs Going away for the week-end. Leaving us all on our own.

Miss Gatsby Tch. Tch. Tch.

Basil Ah, yes.

He chuckles bravely.

Miss Tibbs But we know where you're going.

Basil It's only Paignton.

Miss Tibbs takes his arm and pats it reassuringly.

Miss Tibbs Aah! Well have a lovely time.

Miss Tibbs It'll do you good. You need to get away from things.

Basil (*balefully*) Well, we're going together.

Miss Gatsby waves a finger at him.

Miss Gatsby And don't you worry about us.

Basil Oh! All right! Now . . . you know men are coming to do work here?

Miss Tibbs Yes.

Basil So you have to go down to Gleneagles for your din-dins tonight? Ummm?

He mimes eating. The ladies giggle and mime eating too.

Basil And if you need anything, <u>Polly</u> will be in charge.

He starts to exit.

Miss Tibbs Now have a lovely week-end.

Miss Gatsby And don't do anything we wouldn't do.

Basil Just a little breathing, surely!

He smiles winningly and exits into the lobby.

In the lobby

Basil is going behind the reception desk when he notices, lying on it, a drawing of Polly's. He picks this up, and is staring at it with obvious irritation, as Polly comes through from the inner office.

Basil Polly, I've asked you not to leave your sketches about.

Polly comes over to take it. Basil shakes his head.

Basil I'm sorry, but what is this supposed to be ?

Polly Oh, it's just a sketch.

She reaches for it, but Basil keeps it away from her.

Basil But what is it, what are you trying to do, I mean, this is a junk yard isn' it ?

Polly It's not finished.

She reaches for it again.

Basil Well why's it got a collar and tie underneath ?

Polly Can I have it ?

Basil It's very good . . . old soup tins, broken down car, dustbins and mattresses and hoovers . . . and a nice, smart collar and tie underneath. I mean, what's it supposed to <u>be</u> ?!

Polly It's not important, can I have it back ?

Basil surrenders it, grudgingly.

Basil It's irritating. I mean, do you ever <u>sell</u> things like that ?

Polly I sell a few portraits now and again.

Basil Choh !

Polly (*quietly*) I haven't much hope for this one.

Basil picks up some papers.

Basil Would you give me the stapler, please. I mean what is the point of something like that ?

Polly No point.

Basil No <u>point</u> ?

Polly What's the point in being alive ?

Basil Beats me. Stuck with it, I suppose. Will you give me the stapler, please !

Polly gives him the date stamper.

Polly If you don't go on at me.

Basil looks at the date stamper.

Basil The stapler !

Polly Oh, sorry.

She gives it to him.

Basil What's the matter with you ?

Polly I didn't get much sleep last night.

Basil Tch, choh ! I mean we're leaving you in charge.

The telephone rings.
Sybil comes busily through from the inner
office and answers it.

Polly I wasn't doing it to spite you, I promise.

Basil hits the stapler vengefully.

Basil Oh good! Well, you won't feel so tired then, will you?

Sybil is looking at him, the phone in one
hand.

Sybil Basil...

Basil Who is it?

Sybil It's Mr. O'Reilly.

He takes the phone, looking puzzled.

Basil That's odd. Must be about the garden wall.

Sybil Polly!

Basil (*to phone*) Hallo?... Now look here! When are you coming
to finish the wall?! I'm <u>sick</u> and <u>tired</u> of that pile of bricks!!

Sybil goes back into the inner office,
followed by Polly. Basil looks round, sees
Sybil has gone, and whispers urgently into
the mouthpiece.

Basil I told you not to call. You know my wife thinks Stubbs is doing the doors . . . Well, what time will they be here ? . . . Four o'clock ? Is that enough time ? . . . All right, all right, now if there are any problems get Polly to call me, understand ?

He hears Sybil coming through, and re-adopts the masterful manner.

Basil So next week's definite, is it ? Good. We've waited about as long as Hadrian for that wall. No, Hadrian. The Emperor Hadrian . . . oh, it doesn't matter, never mind, I'll explain it next week. Choh.

He rings off rather grandly. Sybil is unimpressed.

Sybil You don't believe that, do you Basil ? We've been waiting four months, why should he do it now ?

Basil Oh, I think he will this time, dear.

Sybil is going to make her point.

Sybil If you'd used Stubbs . . .

Basil We'd have had a huge bill.

Sybil Look ! You pay for what you get. O'Reilly's a cut-price cock-up artist.

Basil is distressed by such wild abuse.

Basil Oh, Sybil !

Sybil With Stubbs, we may pay a little more . . .

Basil A <u>little</u> more ?

Sybil Yes, a little. But he does a really professional job, and he does it when he says he will.

Basil will argue no more. He strikes a pose of lofty dissension.

Sybil You'll see. What time's he getting here ?

Basil Oh, er . . . four o'clock, I think, dear.

Sybil goes to look out of the main entrance.

Sybil And you're going to wear that jacket, are you?

Basil Yes I am, thank you, dear.

Sybil You just haven't a clue, have you?

Basil You wouldn't understand dear, it's called 'style'.

Sybil sees her friends' car drawing up in the forecourt. Waving and smiling, she calls to them.

Sybil Yoo hoo!! They're here, Basil!

Basil Oh, how fabulous!

She hurries back towards him.

Sybil Now do try and be agreeable this week-end, Basil.

Sybil Now have I got everything?

Basil (*pianissimo*) Handbag, knuckle dusters, flick knife, strychnine . . .

Satisfied, she goes to the main entrance.

Sybil Now come on, Basil, do get a move on !

She disappears down the steps.

Basil Just coming ,dear !

He follows her, puts on a cap, and hovers until she is out of sight. Then he nips back into the lobby.

Basil Polly !

Polly comes out of the inner office.

Polly Yes ?

Basil Now, the men will be here at four o'clock. You know what they're doing ?

Polly Well they're putting a door through to the kitchen . . .

Basil (*prompting*) At the foot of the stairs. And . . .

Polly . . . And . . . ?

Basil (*irritated*) Blocking the <u>drawing room door</u>.

Polly ... Blocking it ?

Basil Yes, blocking it off, girl ! So we can get a bit of privacy away from the plebs. Don't you take anything in ? Where's my cap ?

He looks around for it.

Polly It's on your ...

Basil (*casually*) Oh, and one other thing. They won't be Stubbs' men, they'll be O'Reilly's. Where is that cap ?

He prowls off looking for it.

Polly ... O'Reilly ! ?

Basil Yes, yes ! !

Polly Does Mrs. Fawlty know ?

Basil I don't know, probably not. Don't mention it though, they don't quite hit it off.

Polly But ...

Basil (*rattily*) I had to change it. Stubbs has got a virus or something.

Polly . . . She said you were never to use him again. I don't want to be responsible for . . .

Basil He's sending his best men, all you've got to do is take a look when they've finished. Any problems, ring me. Have a nice week-end.

Polly If she asks me, I'll tell her.

Basil Thank you, thank you so much, Polly. I've always admired loyalty.

Basil exits. Manuel enters. Then he remembers something. He rushes to the desk, finds the golf shoes, and runs after Basil with them. But the car drives off. He returns, crestfallen. Polly is pinning up her drawing on the notice board.

Manuel I forget.

He stares at the drawing for a moment.

Manuel Oh! Mr. Fawlty!

Polly Keep it quiet.
Ventanas, por favour!

Manuel scampers off.

In the lobby, later that day

Manuel Oh, Polly, finish, I <u>tired</u>.

Polly Nearly, Manuel, just hold that a second . . .

Manuel Que ?

She continues to put the finishing touches to the sketch.

Polly Now Manuel. Quiero ascender para dormir.

Manuel No, no. You must speak me English. Is good. I learn.

Polly Manuel, I want to go upstairs.

Manuel Que ?

Polly (*pointing*) I . . . go upstairs . . .

Manuel Si. Is easy.

Polly For a little sleep.

Manuel Is difficult.

Polly For siesta.

Manuel Ah, <u>siesta</u> . . . little sleep ?

Polly Yes.

Manuel Same in Spanish.

Polly When O'Reilly's men come, you wake me.

Manuel Orrible men ! ?

He looks alarmed.

Polly Now, Manuel, listen. When men come . . . Senor O'Reilly . . .

Manuel Men come.

Polly Yes.

She scans the finished drawing and stretches.

Polly Yes. You come upstairs and wake me, despierte me.

She crosses the lobby, yawning.

Manuel Ah ! When men come I . . . vendre arriba para despertartle en su cuarto.

Polly <u>Antes</u> que ellos comienzan trabajar aqui.

Polly finishes.

She disappears upstairs.

Manuel relaxes from his pose. Dutifully, he moves round behind the reception desk and stands there. After a moment he starts enjoying his increased responsibility. He preens himself, struts about a little behind the desk, rings the desk bell in an imperious manner and picks up the telephone, although it has not rung.

Manuel Manuel Towers. How are you. Is nice day. Goodbye.

He rings off as he sees someone arriving.

Manuel Hallo! How are you?

The delivery man finds the delivery note.

Delivery Man Number sixteen?

Manuel consults the hotel register.

Manuel Si, si. Sixteen. But no eat.

Delivery Man What?

Manuel Sixteen is free. But not possible . . .

He mimes eating. The deliveryman stares at him, then deliberately, he indicates the hotel.

Delivery Man Is this . . . number sixteen ?

Manuel No, no, this . . . lobby. Sixteen upstairs, on right.

A pause.

Delivery Man Who's in charge here ?

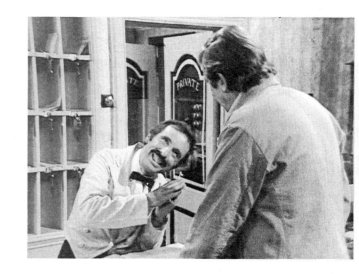

Manuel Charge later. After sleep.

Delivery Man No, no. Where's the boss ?

Manuel He, er . . . I boss.

Delivery Man No, no, where's the real boss ?

Manuel Que ?

Delivery Man The . . . the generalissimo.

Manuel In Madrid.

Delivery Man Oh, just sign this.

He gives Manuel the delivery note and a pencil. Manuel signs it, and gives it back.

Manuel Sixteen?

Delivery Man What?

Manuel You want room sixteen.

Delivery man No, I don't want a room, mate, I'm just leaving him.

He points at the gnome and walks out.

Manuel You want room sixteen . . . for <u>him</u>!?

The delivery man calls over his shoulder.

Delivery man Yeah, with a bath, you dago twit.

Manuel is stunned. Then he calls after him.

Manuel You mad! You . . . <u>mad</u>! —— You pay for room first.

He comes round the desk and picks up the gnome, shaking his head.

Manuel Where I put you? No pay, no room sixteen.

He carries the gnome behind the reception desk and puts it down. The telephone rings. As Manuel goes to answer it O'Reilly's men enter through the main doors.

Manuel (*to phone*) Hallo, Fawlty Towers. How are you, is nice day . . . No, he not here . . . No, no, he <u>not</u> here, very sorry, goodbye.

He replaces the receiver crisply, and looks at the men standing by the desk. There are three of them, Lurphy, Jones, and Kerr. Jones has a plan to which he is referring as he looks round the lobby.

Manuel Hallo, men.

Lurphy Good day, now.

He is Irish.

Manuel You are men?

Lurphy (*dangerously*) . . . What?

Manuel . . . You are men ?

Lurphy takes a threatening half-pace forward.

Lurphy Are you trying to be funny ?

Manuel What . . . ?

Lurphy I said ''Are you trying to be funny ?''

Kerr and Jones lay restraining hands on him.

Kerr Not here, Spud, not here.

Manuel is taken aback.

Manuel But, you are men with Orelly ?

Jones . . . What ?

Manuel You are Orelly men ?

Lurphy steps forward again, menacingly.

Lurphy What does <u>that</u> mean ?

Manuel You Orelly.

He waves a threatening finger at Manuel. Manuel recoils.

Manuel . . . Where Orelly ?

Jones What's he on about ?

Kerr He means O'Reilly.

Understanding is vouchsafed to Lurphy. It is a delightful experience. He beams.

Lurphy Oh yes, we're Orelly men. Ha, ha, ha, ha! Ha ha ha ha! Ha ha ha!

He smiles to Manuel, leans closer to his companions and mutters to them.

Lurphy Thick as a plank.

Manuel addresses them.

Manuel You wait here, please. I go. . . .

He indicates upstairs. The telephone rings. Manuel answers it.

Manuel (*to phone*) You wait too, please.

He replaces the receiver, hurries across the lobby and disappears up the stairs.

In a corridor upstairs

Manuel hurries along towards the door of Polly's Room. He arrives and knocks. There is no sound inside. He knocks again. Still nothing. He opens the door quietly and looks round it.

In Polly's room

Polly is on the bed, asleep. Manuel comes up to her and whispers.

Manuel Polly . . . Polly.

She is in a very deep sleep and so . . .

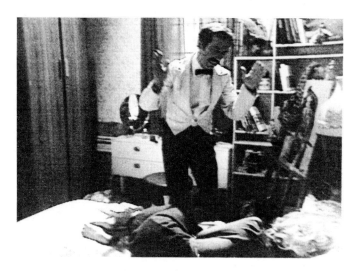

. . . he decides to take care of things himself.

In the lobby

The men are looking around and Jones is examining the dining-room door. The telephone is ringing. Manuel comes running down the stairs and rushes to the telephone.

Manuel Hallo, Fawlty Towers, how are you, is nice day . . . is you again! Oh I tell you, he not here, very, very sorry, goodbye (*he rings off*) Choh! Choh!

The three men are all consulting Jones' plan.

Manuel. You know what to do, men?

Jones Yes, I think so. This is the dining-room?

Manuel nods. They go back to the plan. Manuel watches anxiously.

Manuel . . . You certain you know?

Jones Yes, this looks pretty straightforward. We've just got to block this one off.

The telephone rings again. Manuel picks it up.

Manuel Yes, yes, yes!...Is you again! Listen! I tell you he not here!!! Where are your ears?! You big...hhhhalf wit, I tell you, he <u>not</u> <u>here</u>. Listen!

He holds the receiver at arms length so that the caller may register the lack of Basilic noises. Then he puts it back to his ear. Suddenly, a look of horror passes across his face.

Manuel Oh, Mr. Fawlty, I so <u>sorry</u>! I <u>so</u> <u>sorry</u>!!

Manuel (*to phone*)...Yes, I am here!...No, no, Polly is...very busy...Men? Yes, yes, the men are here...Yes...Man with beard?

Manuel calls to the men.

Manuel Please, which is man with beard?

Quite soon Lurphy indicates himself and comes over.

Manuel . . . yes . . . hid . . . o . . . angtang . . . tag . . . tang . . . si . . . one moment please . . .

He puts the receiver down and addresses Lurphy.

Manuel You are a hid . . . eous . . . orang . . . tang.

He bows. Lurphy hits him.

Basil Well done, Manuel. Thank you.

The dialling tone is heard.

In the forecourt of Fawlty Towers

*It is a lovely morning. Birds are singing ;
moles frolic ; weasels dance the hornpipe*

In Polly's room

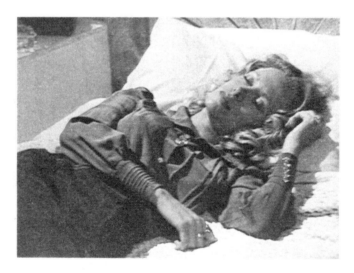

In the forecourt

*Basil's car draws up. Basil leaps out and
runs up the steps.*

In the lobby

Basil strides in

Basil Polly!

He goes to the wall by the stairs where the door through to the kitchen should now be.

It isn't.

He closes his eyes and breathes deeply. He looks round to the door of the drawing-room to see if it is blocked off.

No, it isn't.

He shakes his head in disbelief.

Basil Polly! Polly!!

He turns, opens the door, which has been installed across the foot of the stairs and runs up the stairs.

Basil ... Polly!!!

Basil <u>Manuel</u>!!!!

He makes for the dining room. But the door has gone.

Polly has come downstairs.

Basil What have you done to my hotel?! Polly!!

Polly (*innocently*) What?

Basil What have you done to my hotel ? !

Polly What ?

*He grabs her by the ear and shows her
the new door.*

Basil Look !

Polly Oh, it's nice. I like it there, it's interesting.

*She is led, lobe first, to the late dining
room door.*

Polly Ouch, you're hurting me.

She escapes the ear-lock.

Basil Come on, where's the door ? !
What have you done with it ?

Polly I don't know.

Basil <u>Why</u> don't you know ? ! I left <u>you</u> in charge.

Polly . . . I fell asleep.

Basil You fell <u>asleep</u> ! !

Polly It's not my fault.

Basil You fell <u>asleep</u>, and it's <u>not</u> <u>your</u> <u>fault</u> ! ! ? ?

Polly He forgot to wake me.

A pause.

Basil Who forgot to wake you ?

Polly . . . . . . It <u>is</u> my fault.

Basil Manuel!!!

He lopes about.

Basil Manuel!!!!!!!!

Polly tries to intercede.

Polly Please don't blame him.

Basil (*not unfairly*) Why not?

Polly . . . It wasn't really his fault.

Basil hits the reception desk.

Basil Well whose fault is it then, you cloth-eared bint?! Denis Compton's?!!!

Polly Well, you hired O'Reilly didn't you?

Basil's eyes go oddly glazed.

A pause.

Polly We all warned you. . . . Who else would do something like this ?

She indicates the doors.

Basil . . . I beg your pardon.

Polly You hired O'Reilly . . .

Basil . . . Oh! Oh, I see! Of course! . . . It's my fault isn't it? . . . There I was, thinking it was your fault because you had been left in charge, or Manuel's fault for not waking you up, and all the time it was my fault. Now I understand! I've seen the light. Ah well, if it's my fault, I must be punished then, mustn't I?

Basil You're a naughty boy! Don't do it again!

He catches himself a real cracker across the head, staggers, and straightens up.

Basil There! That'll teach me. Now . . .

He takes a deep breath and starts trembling.

Basil ... What am I going to do? She'll be back at one!!

Polly Now ...

Basil I'm a dead man, do you realise!

Polly (*soothingly*) Easy! ...

Basil You're dead too. We're <u>all</u> <u>dead</u>!!

He is quivering hard.

Polly Don't panic.

Basil What <u>else</u> is there to do?

Polly Listen. We'll call O'Reilly.

But Basil does not take this in. He has started to gibber. Polly shakes him.

Polly Just pull yourself together.

His condition worsens. Polly shakes him harder.

Polly Come on! Come on!

The quivering and gibbering reach a climax. Polly pauses, takes a step back and slaps him in the face.

Basil . . . Again!

She slaps him again, rather deferentially.

Basil Harder!!

Basil Right! I'll call O'Reilly.

*He runs round behind the reception desk
and disappears with a cry.*

Basil What is this ?! What is
going on here ?!

Polly Your wife ordered it. Call O'Reilly.

Basil What ? That golfing puff adder . . .

*He slams the gnome down on the desk
and starts strangling it.*

Polly Call O'Reilly !

Basil What?

Polly Shall I call him?

Basil releases the gnome, grabs the telephone and dials.

Basil No, I'll do it. Leave it to me. Thank you. You go and see if the roof's still on.

Basil ... What, what, what, what ...?

Polly keeps sketching.

Polly I'm just ... er ... keep still!

Basil You can't do that now!!

Polly Hold it, hold it.

Basil Go and see if they've started breakfast! ... Now!!

Polly completes her lightning portrait.

Polly Right.

She hurries off with it. Basil stiffens.

Basil (*silkily*) Hallo, Mr. O'Reilly, and how are you ... Good, good, no rare diseases or anything? Oh good, I'm delighted ... Oh, I do beg your pardon, Basil Fawlty, you know, the poor sod you do jobs for.

Basil . . . Well now, how are things your end . . . Good. Well now, how would you like to hear about things my end . . . Oh, well up to your usual standard I think I could say, a few holes in the wall, the odd door missing, but nothing you can't be sued for.

Manuel trots into the lobby, and sees Basil.

Manuel Good morning.

Basil (*to Manuel*) . . . I beg your pardon ?

Manuel Good morning !

Basil (*to the phone*) One moment.

He puts the receiver down on the desk and walks round to Manuel

Basil Did you say ''Good Morning ?''

Manuel Si.

Basil I see. What are you going to do now then ?

Manuel Que ?

Basil What . . . you . . . do . . . now ?

Manuel I serve breakfast.

Basil Ah ! Let's see you then.

Manuel turns away and starts looking for the dining-room door. After a time, he turns back.

Manuel Where is door ?

Basil Ah ha !

Manuel Is gone.

Manuel points to the wall.

Manuel Door was here.

Basil Where ?

*He picks Manuel up and bangs him
against the wall in three different places.*

Basil Here ? . . . Or here ?

Basil . . . Or here ?

*Manuel droops. The Major enters and
strolls up to them.*

Major Morning, Fawlty.

Basil Good morning, Major. I'm so sorry, but the door seems to have
disappeared.

Major Oh, yes. So it has.

Basil I'm afraid I was silly enough to leave the hotel for a few minutes and . . .

Major Well, not to worry, these things happen.

Major I wonder where it's got to ?

Major Well, it's bound to turn up. . . Er, newspapers arrived, yet ?

Basil Not yet, no, Major. Manuel !

Manuel Si ?

Basil Would you please show the Major how to get into the dining-room via the kitchen ?

Manuel . . . Is difficult.

Basil Major, will you show Manuel how to get into the dining-room via the kitchen ?

Major Certainly. This way ... er ... Manuel.

Basil picks up the phone again.

Basil O'Reilly? ... Now look. I want my dining-room door put back in and the other door taken out, by <u>one o'clock</u>, you understand? ... No, I don't want a debate about it. If you're not here in twenty minutes with my door, I shall come over and insert a large garden gnome in you.

He rings off, with panache.

In the lobby. One hour later.

O'Reilly is nearly at work on the dining-room door.

O'Reilly Well, I'm sorry Mr. Fawlty, my men won't work on a Sunday and that's the way it is.

Basil Well how long's it going to take you?

O'Reilly I'm working as fast as I can.

Basil Well, it had better be fast enough, I mean, she is back in <u>four hours</u>!

Polly comes through the main entrance,
carrying a tray with tea and biscuits on it.

Polly Tea up!

Basil spins round.

Basil What?!

Polly Brewed a cuppa for him, guv.

O'Reilly Lovely!

Basil He hasn't got time to drink that!

But O'Reilly takes the cup before Basil can
intercept it.

Polly Biscuits?

O'Reilly They look good.

Basil No, no. Give them to me (*he confiscates the biscuits*). Now, will
you get on with it!

O'Reilly Look, look! This lot here.

He points to the dining-room door.

O'Reilly An hour and a half. (*He points to the door across the foot of*
the stairs) That one. Off easy. Lick of paint all round, one hour. What's
the time now?

Basil Ten to nine.

O'Reilly All right. Ten to nine and two and a half hours is . . . is . . .
plenty of time. Give us a biscuit.

Basil No. You can have one when you've done that door.

Polly Awwwwwwww.

She exits. O'Reilly goes back to pulling out the nails.

O'Reilly The trouble with you, Mr. Fawlty, is that you <u>worry</u> too much. You keep it up like that you'll have a stroke before you're fifty. Stone dead you'll be.

Basil Suits me.

O'Reilly Oh! That's a dreadful thing to say.

Basil Not at all. Get a bit of peace.

O'Reilly Don't be so morbid. The Good Lord made the world so that we could enjoy ourselves.

Basil My wife enjoys herself. I worry.

O'Reilly I tell you, if the Lord had meant us to worry, he'd have given us things to worry about.

Basil He <u>has</u>! My <u>wife</u>!! She will be back in four hours and she can kill a man at ten paces with one blow of her tongue.

Basil How am I supposed not to worry?

O'Reilly (*calmly*) Just remember Mr. Fawlty; there's always somebody worse off than yourself.

Basil Is there? Well I'd like to meet him. I could do with a laugh.

O'Reilly Well, you'll have to worry for the both of us, Mr. Fawlty. Let me tell you, if the Good Lord . . .

Basil Is mentioned <u>once</u> more, I shall move you closer to him. Now, <u>please</u> . . .

There is a moment's silence as O'Reilly gets another nail out and starts pulling the hardboard away at the top of the door. Polly runs in.

Polly Mr. Fawlty!

Polly . . . She's here!

Basil Oh God.

In the forecourt

In the lobby

Basil Hide!! Hide!!

Basil Hide ! ! I'll try and get rid of her. Hide ! ! ! !

O'Reilly Where ?

Basil points into the bar.

Basil In there !

O'Reilly runs into the cocktail bar.

Polly Mr. Fawlty !

Basil I'll try and stall her.

Polly But . . .

Basil God help me !

Basil runs out of the main entrance.

In the forecourt

Basil Hallo, dear !

Sybil Hallo, Basil.

Basil Well, you finished your golf early !

He tries to engage her on the bottom step but she walks past him.

Sybil We haven't started, Basil.

Basil Where are you going ?

Sybil Up these steps.

Basil Oh, don't do that ! It's such a lovely day.

Basil Let's go for a walk.
We haven't done that for <u>years</u>.

He realises she is not going to stop.

Basil Oh Sybil, I nearly forgot! You'll never believe this.

He scampers after her.

Sybil I think I will.

In the lobby

Basil manages to get through the doors ahead of her.

Basil Let me show you!

He gestures dramatically at the construction fiasco.

Basil There!... look at that! That's Stubbs for you.

Basil Mind you, I warned you! But <u>still</u> ... a reputable company like that. Choh! Tch, tch, tch.

Basil sneaks a quick glance at her and looks straight back to the cock-up.

    Basil Tch, tch, tch.

    Sybil . . . Stubbs ?

He sighs sadly.

    Basil Wicked. Tch !

    Sybil Where's O'Reilly, Basil ?

    Basil (*to himself*) Criminal ! . . . .(*to Sybil*) Hmmm ?

    Sybil Where's O'Reilly ?

    Basil (*uncomprehendingly*) . . . O'Reilly ?

    Sybil Yes, O'Reilly.

Basil stares, then he shakes his head.

Basil Sybil, you never cease to amaze me. Just because of this . . . you automatically assume that it has to be O'Reilly. You just <u>assume</u> that I have been lying to you all along! I mean . . .

He gestures helplessly.

Basil . . . <u>Why</u> . . . O'Reilly?

Sybil Because his van's outside.

Basil Well, he's here <u>now</u>!

Basil Of course he's here <u>now</u>!! He's come to clear up this mess that your Stubbs has made. That's why his (*suddenly screaming*) VAN'S OUTSIDE!!!

He controls himself.

Basil On a Sunday. That's what I call service.

Sybil I agree.

Basil . . . You do?

Sybil Yes. But if Stubbs has made this mess I think he should come and clear it up.

Basil Well, there's no point now that O'Reilly's here. We want it done <u>straight</u> <u>away</u>.

Sybil There's no point in paying money to Mr. O'Reilly when Stubbs would have to do it for free. I'll call him now.

She makes for the phone.

Basil He won't be there on a Sunday.

Sybil I'll call him at home.

Basil is suddenly racked by a spasm of pain from his old war wound.

Basil Aaaaaaaaaaggh!

Sybil stops. Basil grasps his thigh and moans.

Basil Ooooh! Damm leg's giving me a lot of gyp this morning. Not to worry. Anyway, I've called him at home and he's not there.

Sybil When did you call him?

Basil First thing. Before I tried O'Reilly.

Sybil Wasn't that rather early? For a Sunday.

Basil <u>And</u> I called him five minutes ago, just before you came in. Nobody there. Aagh!

*He flexes his leg. The telephone rings.
He answers it.*

Basil Yes, hallo, Fawlty Towers, yes?!

Basil . . . Who??!!

A new development. Hope dawns.

Basil Oh! Yes, yes, yes! Well, I think you'd better speak to my wife.

He offers her the receiver.

Basil (*matter-of-factly*) It's someone from Stubbs's, dear.

Sybil looks dubious but takes the phone.

Sybil Hallo, Sybil Fawlty? Oh yes . . . Yes, well it is a complete mess. Can you come over straight away and put it right?

Sybil You handle this, Basil.

She gives the phone back, smiles sweetly, and walks off.

In the drawing-room

Polly So we're very busy for at least three weeks . . .

Polly So if you want it done straight away, you'd better try someone like . . . oh, what's his name . . . ?

Sybil O'Reilly?

Polly winces and puts her tail between her legs.

Basil's voice comes over the phone.

Basil Bravo, Polly. Well done girl! But where are you speaking from??

Sybil takes the phone.

Sybil She's in here with me, Basil.

Sybil replaces the receiver, rises, and makes for the door.

Polly Mrs. Fawlty, it's partly my fault.

Sybil No it isn't.

In the lobby

The drawing-room door opens and Sybil emerges, half-followed by Polly. Basil is shouting into the telephone.

Basil Is that someone there pretending to be from Mr. Stubbs' Company ?!!

Basil What sort of game do you think you're playing ?!! I mean <u>really</u>!!

He slams the phone down and turns to Sybil.

Basil Would you believe what some people will do ?

Sybil I am going to make you regret this for the rest of your life, Basil.

Basil nods.

Basil Fair enough, I suppose. But I think Stubbs is <u>partly</u> . . .

Sybil (*screaming*) Basil !!!!

Basil leaps in the air, lands and withdraws a couple of paces.

Basil ... Yes, dear?

Sybil Don't you <u>dare</u>!!! Don't you dare give me any more of those ... pathetic lies!!

Basil Oh! Right.

Sybil What do you <u>take</u> me for?!! Did you really think I could believe this shambles was the work of professional builders, people who do this for a <u>living</u>?

Basil looks at the work.

Basil No, not really, no.

Sybil <u>Why</u> did I <u>trust</u> you, Basil?! <u>Why</u> did I let you <u>make</u> the arrangements?! I could have seen what was going to happen. <u>Why</u> did I <u>do</u> it?!

Basil ... Well, we all make mistakes, dear.

Sybil runs to the reception desk.

Sybil I am <u>sick to death</u> of you!!! You never learn, do you?! You <u>never</u>, <u>ever</u>, <u>learn</u>!!!

She picks up the cash box.

In the cocktail bar

In the lobby

Basil is backing off. Sybil pursues him.

Sybil We've used O'Reilly three times this year and each time it's been a <u>fiasco</u>!! That wall out there is <u>still</u> not done!! You got him in to change a washer in November and we didn't have any running water for <u>two days</u>!!

Basil (*reasonably*) Well, he's not really a plumber, dear.

Sybil Well, <u>why</u> did you <u>hire</u> him?!

Basil chews this over.

Sybil . . . Because he's <u>cheap</u>!

Basil Oh, I wouldn't call him cheap, Sybil.

Sybil Well . . . what would you call him ?

Basil (*weighing his words*) Cheap . . . ish.

Sybil And the reason he's cheap is he's no bloody good!

Basil Oh, Sybil, you do exaggerate. I mean, he's not brilliant . . .

Sybil Not brilliant ! ? ! ? ! ?

Sybil He belongs in a zoo ! ! !

She kicks him on the shin. He hops about.

Basil Sybil, you never give anybody the benefit of the doubt.

She kicks his other shin.

O'Reilly appears in the background.

Sybil He's shoddy, he doesn't care, he's a liar . . . he's lazy, he's incompetent, he's a half-witted thick Irish joke ! !

Basil Hallo, O'Reilly ! There you are. How funny ! We were just talking about you .

Basil And then we got on to <u>another</u> Irish builder we used to know, God, he was awful!

Sybil I was talking about you, Mr. O'Reilly.

Basil (*taken aback*) . . . <u>Were</u> you ? I thought you were . . .

He puts his hand on Sybil's arm to calm her a little. She slaps it hard. He takes it away and comforts it. O'Reilly takes over, with his gentle Irish charm.

O'Reilly Now, come, come, Mrs. Fawlty . . .

She walks over to him.

Sybil I'm coming.

O'Reilly (*winningly*) Oh dear me, what have I done now ?

Sybil points to his work.

Sybil That and that.

He puts a hand on her arm.

O'Reilly Not to worry. I'm putting it right.

Sybil . . . Not to worry ?

O'Reilly You've heard of the genius of the lamp, Mrs. Fawlty ? That's me.

Sybil . . . You think I'm joking, don't you ?

Basil Oh, <u>don't</u> smile.

Sybil . . . Why are you smiling, Mr. O'Reilly ?

O'Reilly Well, to be perfectly honest . . . I like a woman with spirit.

Sybil Oh, <u>do</u> you ? Is <u>that</u> what you like ?

O'Reilly I do, I do.

Sybil Oh good.

She picks a golfing umbrella out of the stand.
Basil steps forward.

Basil Now, Sybil ! That's enough.

She hits him with it.

Basil That's enough !

Sybil steps up to the apprehensive O'Reilly and whacks him. He steps back , alarmed.

Sybil *(encouragingly)* Come on ! Give us a smile.

She wallops him.

Sybil Give us a smile.

O'Reilly disappears under a flurry of blows, emitting a charming gentle Irish cry of distress.
Sybil lowers the umbrella and stands over him.

Sybil O'Reilly. I have seen more intelligent creatures than you lying on their backs at the bottom of ponds. I have seen better organised creatures running around farmyards with their heads cut off. Now collect your stuff and get out.

She walks over to the phone at reception, and starts dialling.

Sybil I never want to see you or any of your men in my hotel again. Now if you'll excuse me, I have to speak to a professional builder.

She finishes dialling and waits. O'Reilly, rather stunned, crawls slowly to collect his equipment. Basil smiles supportively at him.

Sybil (*briskly*) Hallo. Mr. Stubbs ? . . . It's Sybil Fawlty. I'm sorry to disturb you on a Sunday, but we have a problem with a couple of doors that we'd like you to take care of. When do you think you could come and take a look ?

Sybil Nine o'clock tomorrow morning ? . . . Yes, that's fine. See you then. Thank you very much. Goodbye.

She rings off and turns to Basil. He gets a twinge from his war wound.

Sybil Well, I think I shall go over to Audrey's now. I shan't be back till the morning.

She picks up her golf shoes, and starts to move to the door. She sees the gnome.

Sybil Oh, Basil ?

Basil Yes dear ?

Sybil What is that doing here ?

Basil It's a garden gnome, dear.

Basil (*warmly*) Isn't it nice ?

Sybil Do you think it would go better in the garden ?

Basil Yes, dear. Good idea !

*He hurries across, picks it up and smiles at
Sybil. She looks thoughtful.*

Sybil No, no, Basil. On second thoughts, put him back. I think I'll leave
him in charge. I'm sure he's cheap, and he's certainly more use than
you.

*She turns on her heel and exits. Basil
stares after her. Then he calls.*

Basil Have a nice day ! Don't drive over any mines or anything. (*To
himself*) Toxic midget.

*He turns, to see O'Reilly making for the
main entrance with his bundle of tools.*

Basil . . . Er ! ! . . . Where are <u>you</u> going, O'Reilly ?

O'Reilly checks his stride.

O'Reilly Well, I . . .

Basil Well take your tools back and continue with the work, please.

O'Reilly . . . Well, in view of what Mrs. Fawlty was saying, I thought. . .

Basil saunters nonchalantly over to him.

Basil You're not going to take that seriously, are you?

O'Reilly Well, I thought I might.

Basil You <u>thought</u> you <u>might</u>?!!

O'Reilly Er . . .

Basil What sort of man are you, O'Reilly? . . . Are you going to let her speak to us like that?

O'Reilly . . . She did Mr. Fawlty!

Basil No, she didn't. She thinks she did, but we'll show her. We're not <u>just</u> going to put this door back and take that one out, we're going to close that one up and put that one in as well.

Basil We're going to do the best day's work you've ever done, O'Reilly.

In the lobby. The next morning.

The lobby has been totally renovated. The dining-room has been restored; the door across the stairs is gone; a new door has been created, leading to the kitchen; and the door to the drawing-room has been blocked off. Everything has been made good and painted. The effect is pleasing.

Polly is giving a final polish to the drawing-room ex-door. Manuel is standing by the main doors looking outside. Basil appears through the new kitchen door and makes his way across to reception.

> **Basil** Manuel! Any sign?

> **Manuel** Que? No, no, no.

He continues to watch the forecourt. The Major comes down the stairs.

> **Major** Morning, Fawlty.

> **Basil** Morning, Major. Papers are here.

> **Major** Ah, good.

> **Basil** Notice anything new, Major?

> **Major** Another car strike!

Basil . . . Never mind.

The Major strolls over to the dining-room door. Polly is there giving it the quick once over.

Polly Good morning, Major.

Major Good morning, er . . .

He looks at her.

Polly . . . Never mind.

He looks at the door.

Major Ah, you found it!

Major I knew you would. (*To Polly*) He lost it, you know.

He goes into the dining room.

Manuel She come!!

Basil Quick!

Basil Morning, dear!

Basil Did you have a good evening dear?

Mr. Stubbs arrives punctually.

Basil Ah, Mr. Stubbs! My wife's just over there.

He disappears into the inner office.

Stubbs Good morning, Mrs. Fawlty.

Sybil turns to greet him. She looks most discomfited.

Sybil Oh, Mr. Stubbs, this is most awkward . . . I'm afraid I have to apologise.

Basil appears briefly from the inner office whistling cheerfully. He disappears again. Sybil smiles apologetically.

Sybil My husband has put me in a rather embarrassing situation . . . once again. I <u>was</u> going to ask you to do some work here . . .

Stubbs . . . Yes ?

Sybil But I was away last night and when I got back just now . . . well, it appears to have been done . . .

Basil Everything all right, dear ?

Sybil ignores him.

Stubbs Oh, I see.

Sybil I mean it'll probably all fall down by lunch but . . .

Basil joins them.

Basil Oh, do you think so, dear ? Well, let's ask a real <u>expert</u>.

Basil Do <u>you</u> think it'll all fall down by lunch. Mr. Stubbs ?

Stubbs No no . . .

Basil No, Mr. Stubbs doesn't agree with you on <u>that</u> one, dear.

Stubbs (*peering*) . . . It's a very good job.

Basil Did you hear that, dear ? . . . A very good job.

Sybil Hmmm ?

Basil Oh, none of us like to be wrong, dear. I certainly don't.

Basil We knocked this one through, and closed that one off.

Stubbs What did you use, an RSJ?

Basil No. Four by two.

Basil Not bad, eh, dear? And <u>not</u> expensive.

Stubbs No, I mean for the lintel.

Basil looks round at Stubbs.

Stubbs Did you use an RSJ ? . . . You know, an iron girder ? Or a concrete lintel ?

Basil . . . No, a wooden one.

Stubbs But it's a supporting wall !

Sybil What ? !

Basil <u>Quite</u>. Well thanks very much for coming over.

Sybil Wait a moment!

Sybil You mean that it isn't strong enough?

Stubbs is looking up, apprehensively.

Stubbs This is a supporting wall, Mrs. Fawlty. That could give way any moment.

Sybil Any moment?!

Stubbs Yes, God help the floors above!

He closes the kitchen door.

Stubbs Look, keep this door shut until I get a screwjack to prop it up.

He hurries across to the telephone.

Stubbs Before the whole bloody thing collapses!

Sybil Basil!!

In the forecourt

Sybil Basil!!! Where are you going!!

Basil I'm going to see Mr. O'Reilly, dear.

Basil Then I think I might go to Canada.

THE HOTEL INSPECTORS

CAST

Basil Fawlty .... John Cleese

Sybil Fawlty .... Prunella Scales

Polly .... Connie Booth

Manuel .... Andrew Sachs

Hutchison .... Bernard Cribbins

Walt .... James Cossins

John .... Geoffrey Morris

Brian .... Peter Brett

Major Gowen .... Ballard Berkeley

Miss Tibbs .... Gilly Flower

Miss Gatsby .... Renee Roberts

In the office

Basil is hard at work

At the reception desk

Sybil Yes . . . Yes . . . well it all started
with that electrician didn't it . . . a real
live wire he was, only one watt but
plenty of volts as they say . . .

*She laughs – machine gun plus seal bark.
The noise rattles Basil. He puts a cigarette
in his mouth and looks in vain for a match.
Sybil has taken them.*

Sybil Well anything in trousers, yes . . . or out of them preferably
(*She laughs*) Yes . . . um . . . no, just lighting up, go on.

*Basil gets to his feet and moves to
reception.*

Sybil Yes . . . yes, I'd heard that, with
her mother in the same room.

Basil takes the matches. Sybil takes them back, opens the box, takes one out and gives it to him. Basil is disgruntled but sees a guest approaching reception and skips smartly back into the inner office.

Sybil No, no, of course I won't, go on.

The new arrival, Mr. Hutchison, stops at the desk. Sybil sees him.

Sybil Basil!

Basil has sat down.

Basil Yes dear?

Sybil Oh no!... Who saw them? <u>Basil</u>!

Basil (*trying to strike his match on the desk*). Yes dear?

Sybil Would you come and attend to a gentleman out here, dear?...
(*To phone*) <u>Nineteen</u>?

Basil What, you mean, out where you are, dear?

Sybil Well the last one was only twenty-two... he <u>was</u>!

Basil Actually I'm quite busy in here dear... are you very busy out there?

Sybil I'm on the telephone, Basil. (*To Hutchison*) My husband will be with you in a moment.

Basil So I'll stop working and come and help out there, shall I?

Sybil No, no, no, the Maltese one.

Basil Well I'm glad that's settled then.

Basil gets up reluctantly.

In reception

Basil enters.

Sybil No, no dear, <u>he</u> was an Arab.

Basil Darling, when you're finished . . . why don't you have a lie-down?

He moves on to Hutchison.

Basil I'm sorry to have kept you waiting. I had no idea my wife was so busy.

Hutchison Fear not, kind sir, it matters not one whit.

Basil . . . I beg your pardon.

Hutchison (*loudly*) It matters not one whit, time is not pressing on me fortunately. Now some information please. This afternoon I shall be visiting the town for sundry purposes which would certainly be of no interest to you I am sure, but I shall nevertheless require you to aid me in arranging some form of transport, some hired vehicle, that is, to my first port of call.

Basil Are you all right?

Hutchison Oh I find the air here most invigorating.

Basil I see . . . Did I gather from your last announcement that you want a taxi?

Hutchison In a nutshell.

Basil (*turning away*) Case more like.

He picks up a minicab card.
Sybil finishes her call and takes her coffee
into the office.

Hutchison (*firmly*) At two o'clock please.

Basil (*giving him the card*) Here's the number of the local firm.

Hutchison Will you do it for me please. I never use the telephone if I can avoid it.

Basil Why not?

Hutchison The risk of infection . . . Now. I have a rendezvous at five o'clock at this address which I must reach from the Post Office in Queen's Parade, so as this map is sadly inadequate would you be so good as to draw me a diagram of the optimum route?

Basil Can I ask what's wrong with the map ?

Hutchison It's got curry on it.

Basil . . . Look it's perfectly simple, you go to the end of Queen's Parade, bear left . . .

Hutchison rudely waves the pen and paper in Basil's face.

Basil . . . Look, just <u>listen</u>.

Hutchison I'd rather have the diagram.

Basil It really is very simple.

Hutchison No. I'd rather have the diagram if it doesn't put you out.

Basil It does put me out.

Hutchison Well I'd like it anyway.

Basil looks dangerous.

Sybil Basil!!

Basil (*through clenched teeth*) . . . Right.

Basil starts looking round for paper and pen.

Hutchison (*brandishing his pen at Basil*) Here we are, here we are.

Basil We do have pens, thank you.

Hutchison What?

Basil We have actually got pens in the hotel thank you . . . (*He looks around vainly*) <u>Somewhere</u> . . . I mean <u>where</u> <u>are</u> <u>the</u> <u>pens</u> . . . ?

As Basil looks around furiously, another guest, Walt, a smoothish-looking gentleman in his mid-forties arrives at the desk. Sybil starts checking him in.

Basil Where are the pens?

Basil There are no <u>pens</u> here!
(*To Walt*) I mean can you believe it?
I mean this is <u>supposed</u> to be a <u>hotel</u>.

Sybil is holding a cardboard box out
towards Basil which she has just picked up
from the top of the desk. She shakes it.
It rattles.

Basil . . . Well what are they doing in there?

Sybil I put them there.

Basil Why?

Sybil Would you just sign there, Mr. Walt. Because you're always
losing them, Basil.

Basil I am not always losing them. People take them.

Sybil Well they don't take them from me.

Basil They wouldn't dare.

Basil takes a pen out of the box and starts
drawing the diagram, while muttering . . .

Basil Well, I'm sorry I didn't guess that you'd suddenly done that after twelve years, dear. I'm afraid my psychic powers must be a little below par this morning. (*Pushing the diagram at Hutchison*) There you are.

Sybil Don't be silly Basil, it's written there quite clearly on the top of the box (*shows him, then rings for Manuel*).

Basil (*staring*) . . . ''Pens''? . . . It looks more like ''Bens'' to me.

Sybil (*encouragingly*) Well when Ben comes you can give it to him. Mr. Walt's in room seven.

Basil (*to Walt suddenly*) What do you think? Doesn't that look like ''Bens'' to you?

Walt (*keeping his distance*) . . . Not really.

Basil Well, it does to me (*he takes a pen and alters it*). There. <u>That's</u> a ''P''.

Hutchison (*studying his diagram*) I don't understand this, where is the Post Office?

Basil It's there where it says ''Post Office''. I'm sorry if it is confusing.

Hutchison Oh. ''P.Off.'' You've used the abbreviation.

Basil Ah the penny's dropped.

Hutchison Well I thought it said Boff.

Basil is confirmed in his view of this gentleman's intelligence.

    Basil Of course.

    Hutchison I thought Boff might be the name of a locale . . . you know of the district.

Basil shakes his head to himself.

Hutchison That "P" looks like a "B" you see.

Basil No it doesn't.

Hutchison You see there's a little loop there which . . .

Basil (*taking the diagram and showing it to Walt*) Excuse me. Would you say that was a "P" or a "B" ?

Walt . . . Er . . .

Basil (*pointing*) There. Does it say "Boff" or does it say "Poff" ?

Walt . . . Er . . .

Basil There! There! It's a "P" isn't it ?

Walt (*unwillingly*) I suppose so.

Basil P. Off.

Walt ...I beg your pardon!

Basil P.Off. Not B.Off. Whoever heard of a Bost Office?

Manuel arrives.

Basil (*to Walt*) Nine?

Walt What?

Basil (*as to mental defective*) Room nine?

Walt Seven.

Basil (*to Manuel*) Would you take these cases to room seven.

Manuel Que?

*Basil pauses, then takes some cards from
below the desk. He shows Manuel a
picture of a suitcase.*

> **Basil** (*to Walt, indicating Hutchison*) He thinks Boff is a locale . . .

He shows Manuel a vertical arrow.

> **Walt** He thinks what ?

> **Basil** You know a province . . . some zone in equatorial Torquay.

He shows Manuel a number "Seven".

*Manuel takes Walt's cases and scurries
upstairs with them. Walt follows him.
Hutchison turns to Basil.*

Hutchison I shall be in the lounge if anyone wants me.

Basil . . . If anyone <u>wants</u> you!?

Hutchison Yes. (*Begins to move off*)
In the lounge. (*Exits*)

Basil (*calling after him*) Anyone in particular? . . . I mean Henry
Kissinger? . . . or just anyone with a big net?

In the office

Sybil sits filing her nails.

Basil I don't know what it is about this place . . . the people we get
here . . .

Sybil What are you on about?

Basil (*starting to sharpen pencil*) I wish you'd . . . <u>help</u> a bit. You're
always . . . refurbishing yourself.

Sybil What?

Basil Oh . . . never mind! Never mind!!

Sybil Don't shout at me Basil. I've had a difficult morning.

Basil (*solicitously*) Oh dear, what happened? Did you get entangled in the eiderdown again . . . not enough cream in your eclair? Hmmm? Or did you have to talk to all your friends for so long that you didn't have time to perm your ears . . .

Sybil Actually I've been working, Basil.

Basil Chhhh!

Sybil You know what I mean by ''working'', don't you, dear? I mean getting things done, as opposed to squabbling with the guests.

Basil I would find it a bit easier to deal with some of the cretins we get in here, my little nest of vipers, if I got a smidgeon of co-operation from you.

Sybil Co-operation, that's a laugh. The day you co-operate you'll be in a wooden box. I never heard such rudeness.

Basil Look if you expect me to fawn to some of the yobbos we get in here . . .

Sybil This is a hotel, Basil, not a Borstal, and it might help business if you showed a little courtesy, just a little. (*She rises*).

Basil I suppose talking to Audrey for half an hour helps business.

Sybil It was about business for your information. Audrey has news that might interest you.

Basil Oh this'll be good. Let me guess . . . The Mayor wears a toupee? Somebody's got nail varnish on their cats? Am I getting warm . . . ?

Sybil There are some hotel inspectors in town. (*Exits*).

Basil is stunned. After a moment, he runs after her.

In the lobby

He catches her up.

Basil What ? What does she know ?

Sybil (*calmly*) A friend of Bill Morton's heard three men in a pub last night comparing notes on places they'd just been in Exeter.

Basil Three men ! ? . . . I'll call Bill.

Sybil You don't have to call Bill, Basil. Just try to exercise a little courtesy.

Sybil exits into the kitchen. Basil hovers and then heads rapidly for phone at the reception desk.
Basil is about to pick up the phone when the Major comes in from the bar.

Major Papers arrived yet, Fawlty ?

Basil No, not yet . . . Ah-ha ! <u>So</u> sorry, Major.

Major exits. Basil sees Hutchison approaching again. He pretends not to, and starts dialling. Hutchison, ignored, starts ringing the bell insistently. After several moments, Basil stops dialling and fixes Hutchison with a baleful glare.

Hutchison Could you do that in a moment, please ?

Basil I'm on the telephone.

Hutchison Well you haven't finished dialling yet, have you ?

He puts his finger on the receiver rest, cutting off Basil's call. Basil puts the receiver down. Hutchison gets his finger away in time.

Hutchison Now then . . . there is a documentary tonight on BBC 2 on Squawking Bird, the leader of the Blackfoot Indians in the late 1860's, which commences at eight-forty-five and lasts for three-quarters-of-an hour.

Basil I'm sorry, are you talking to me ?

Hutchison Indeed I am. Is it possible for me to reserve the BBC 2 channel for the duration of this televisual feast ?

Basil Why don't you talk properly ?

Hutchison I beg your pardon ?

Basil No. It isn't.

Hutchison What ?

Basil No, it is <u>not</u> possible to reserve the BBC 2 channel from the commencement of your televisual feast until the moment of the termination of its ending, thank you so much.

*He starts to re-dial, but Hutchison again
puts his finger firmly on the rest.*

Hutchison Well in that case may I suggest you introduce such a
scheme?

Basil No.

*He brings the receiver down hard,
missing the finger by a whisker.*

Hutchison (*inexorably*) It might interest you to learn that I have a
wide experience of hotels and many of them have the foresight to
make arrangements of this kind for the benefit of their guests.

Basil (*unimpressed*) Oh I see, you have a <u>wide</u> experience of hotels
have you?

Hutchison Yes, my professional activities keep me in constant
contact with them.

Basil (*going back to dialling*) Oh do they? Do they really?

*Pause. Basil has registered a potential
connection between Hutchison and ''Hotel
Inspector''.*

Hutchison Well then, am I able to hire a television to watch the
programme in my room?

Basil (*playing for time*) . . . I beg your pardon?

Hutchison Do you have facilities for hiring television sets to your
guests?

Basil Er well . . . Good point. I'm glad you asked me that. Not . . . as
such.

Hutchison Oh.

Basil However, we have plans to introduce such a scheme in the near
future.

Hutchison Well that's not much use to me, is it?

Basil No, but . . . I'll tell you what. Why don't I introduce <u>another</u> scheme right away, along the lines you suggested, by which I reserve the BBC 2 channel for you tonight.

Hutchison Oh well, that's more like it.

Basil Not at all. After all that's what we're here for, isn't it?

Hutchison (*slightly suspicious*) Yes . . .

Basil Is there anything else, before I call your car?

Hutchison Yes. Someone in there mentioned that you have a table tennis table.

Basil Indeed we do. It is not . . . in absolutely mint condition. But it could certainly be used in an emergency.

Hutchison Ah.

Basil It is to be found in the South Wing, just overlooking the courtyard, where there is of course ample parking.

Hutchison What?

Polly has entered the main door and is passing behind them when Basil calls out.

Basil Ah, Polly!

Polly Yes, Mr. Fawlty?

Basil Mr. Hutchison, may I introduce Polly Shearman, who is with us at the moment.

Hutchison Oh . . . how do you do?

Polly How do you do?

Hutchison Wait a minute. We've already met, I think.

Polly Yes, I served you at breakfast.

Hutchison Oh yes. (*Wagging his finger at her*) And you spilt the grapefruit juice, didn't you, you naughty girl?

Polly (*charmingly*) And <u>you</u> moved the glass, didn't you?

Basil (*quickly*) Thank you, thank you, Polly.

Polly moves off.

Basil (*confidentially*) Awfully nice girl. She's very bright. Fully qualified painter, you know.

Hutchison Oh really?

Miss Tibbs and Miss Gatsby come downstairs.

Basil Good morning, ladies.

Miss Tibbs and Miss Gatsby Good morning, Mr. Fawlty.

Basil (*to Hutchison, resuming his theme*) We do like to get girls of that calibre to help us out, it does add a certain . . . Well, would you care to partake of lunch now?

He moves round to usher Hutchison into the dining room.

Hutchison Oh yes, but it's not yet . . .

Basil Oh goodness, we don't worry about things like that here. This is a hotel, not a . . .

Sybil has appeared from the kitchen while Basil has been escorting Hutchison to the dining room.

Sybil Basil ?

Basil Yes dear ?

Sybil It's not half past yet.

Basil I was just saying to Mr. Hutchison dear, this is a hotel not a Borstal. Ha ha ha.

He signals to Sybil and mouths "Inspector".

Sybil is puzzled.
Hutchison goes into the dining room.

Sybil Chef won't be ready Basil.

Basil Leave it to me, dear, leave it to me. (*Continues to signal*).

Sybil Did you ring Bill ?

Basil No dear, not necessary. (*Signals on*).

Sybil What ?

Basil Explain later. (*Winks*). But now I must look after Mr. Hutchison. (*Mouths "Inspector" again*).

In the dining room

Polly is writing Hutchison's order.

Polly One Spanish omelette (*she moves away*).

Hutchison (*loudly*) And all on the plate please, none on the tablecloth.

Polly (*turning back*) . . . Excuse me, you're not by any chance the Duke of Kent are you?

Hutchison No, no . . . oh no. No way.

Basil bustles up.

Basil Ah, Mr. Hutchison! You've ordered, have you?

Hutchison Yes, I'm trying your Spanish omelette.

Basil Excellent.

Hutchison I assume all the vegetables within the omelette are fresh.

Basil Oh yes, yes.

Hutchison (*pointedly*) Including the peas?

Basil Oh yes, they're fresh all right.

Hutchison They're not frozen?

Basil . . . Well they're frozen, yes.

Hutchison Well if they're frozen they're not fresh, are they?

Basil Well I assure you they were perfectly fresh when they were frozen.

Hutchison There's a lot of this nowadays in hotels.

Basil A lot of what?

Hutchison I'll have cheese salad, please.

Basil What?

Hutchison I eat only fresh vegetables, so I'll have the cheese salad instead.

Basil We could do the omelette without the peas.

Hutchison No, I have always regarded the peas as an integral part of the overall flavour so may I suggest that in future you avail yourself of sufficient quantities of the fresh article.

Basil . . . Now look! We've been serving . . . (*recovers himself*) Good idea, yes . . . yes . . . now, something to drink?

Hutchison A ginger beer, please.

Basil A ginger beer?

Hutchison Yes, and a glass of fresh water.

Basil . . . Fresh?

Sybil puts her head round the door.

Sybil Mr. Hutchison. A telephone call for you at reception.

Hutchison Oh dear.

He takes out a clean handkerchief, rises and exits.

Basil (*to himself*) . . . Clever . . .

*Basil hurries out into the kitchen.
Manuel enters from the kitchen and Walt
enters from the lobby.
Walt looks around, wondering where he
should sit, and then looks at Manuel, who is
moving about putting napkins on tables.*

Walt Good afternoon.

Manuel (*still on the move*) No, no, is
no sun. Is not good for me.

Walt I beg your pardon?

Manuel I homesick, yes?

Walt . . . Is there anywhere you'd like me to sit?

Manuel Que?

Walt I'm in room seven.

Manuel Ah, room seven.

*Manuel ushers Walt to the Lobby and
points up the stairs.*

Manuel You go here . . . up . . . (*indicates to the right at the top of the
stairs*) Room seven.

Walt No.

Manuel I show you.

Walt No, no, look. I want a table.

Manuel A table ?

Walt For one.

Manuel Ah ! Table one. Here. (*Indicates a table in the middle of the
room*) Please.

Walt . . . Thank you.

*Manuel now helps Walt to sit and goes and
gets a menu and also a piece of white card.
He gives Walt the menu.*

Manuel (*fluently*) I so sorry, but I
think you say for room and I do it for I
am myself not want to know it easily.

Walt I'm sorry ?

Manuel No. Is my fault.

Walt Well, I'd like the paté . . . and the lamb casserole.

Manuel (*after looking at the white card*) You . . . room ten ?

Walt No. Room <u>seven</u>.

Manuel Seven ?

Walt Yes.

Manuel No, no, <u>this</u> table <u>one</u>. Is Wednesday. Room seven here is table five. Please.

Walt gets up, keeping his cool and goes to table five while Manuel says, with reference to the card . . .

Manuel Seven is what I think you say but one is for table not for this one so is come se habla en Ingles pero puedo ver las nombres solamente quando estan delante de me. (*He laughs a good deal*).

Walt has sat down.

Walt (*stoically*) The paté and the lamb.

Manuel Si. Paté . . . Lamba. (*He turns and walks away muttering*).

The kitchen doors open and Polly comes through, sees Manuel and speaks with a "Write-it-down" gesture.

Polly Escriba – escriba – le.

Manuel Si si. (*Exits into kitchen*).

Basil, who is following close behind Polly, now comes up behind Walt (now happily settled in Hutchison's place). Basil puts the ginger beer and the glass of water down, saying . . .

Basil One ginger beer . . . one glass of fresh water.

He looks at Walt, and jumps in the air.

Basil What are you doing there ?

Walt . . . I . . .

Basil You can't sit there, it's <u>taken</u>. Come on.

Walt I've been moved once already.

Basil Well you're in room seven, aren't you ?

Walt Yes, but the waiter said table five.

Basil Well <u>this</u> isn't table five, is it ? (*sees the plastic table number ; it says "Five"*) Tch. (*picks it up, shaking his head and moves to another table*) Now would you come over here please, this is table five (*puts the "Five" down on the new table and takes an "Eight" off and puts it in his pocket*) . . . Come on !

Walt Look, I did ask the waiter.

Basil Well he's hopeless, isn't he ? You might as well ask the cat. (*Inexcusably*) Now settle down, come on, come on.

Walt . . . I beg your pardon ?

Basil Would you sit down, please ?

Walt, resignedly, sits.

Basil (*making off*) Thank you.

Walt I apologise for taking up more of your time but may I see the wine list?

Basil (*looking back, wearily*) <u>Now</u>?

Walt Yes please.

Basil walks to the Major, removes the wine list from his grasp and returns to Walt.

Basil There you are. Happy now?

Walt Could I have an ashtray?

Basil Oh!

Walt now looks through the wine list while Basil produces an ashtray.

Walt A bottle of the Aloxe-Corton, '67, please.

Basil The what?

Walt (*showing him*) The Aloxe-Corton '67.

Basil (*registering the price*) Oh! The Cor<u>tonne</u>. Yes, of <u>course</u>, my pleasure.

Basil returns the wine list to the Major as Hutchison re-enters the room wiping his ear with his handkerchief.

Basil Ah Mr. Hutchison! Nice to have you back again. We've missed you. (*Fawns after him*).

Hutchison (*who feels a little crowded*) Not so close, please.

Basil gives ground.

Basil I hope all was satisfactory.

Hutchison Your earpiece was extremely greasy but I've wiped it for for you.

Basil Oh thank you, thank you so much.
(*Exits to kitchen*)

Hutchison ceremoniously tastes his ginger beer and announces to the room, as Polly enters from the kitchen . . .

Hutchison It's <u>tepid</u>! Oh <u>dear</u> <u>me</u>!!

Basil comes steaming back in.

Hutchison Ah, you! Do you have an ice bucket, please?

Basil An ice bucket?

Hutchison This ginger beer's distinctly warm.

Basil Polly. An ice bucket for Mr. Hutchison, please. Thank you, Mr. Hutchison.

Polly looks dazed.
Basil arrives at Walt's table and shows him the bottle.

Basil The Cor<u>tonne</u> '67.

Clearly performing for Hutchison, he inserts the corkscrew with panache, and pulls. He struggles, gamely smiles, turns his back, struggles again and it comes. Triumphantly, he pours. Alas, no wine is forthcoming. He re-inserts the corkscrew, struggles, and pours again with the same lack-of-wine problem. Now a dribble flows, followed closely by a torrent. Some goes in the glass.

Basil (*smiling graciously*) Thank you. May I congratulate you on your choice.

Basil makes to leave. Walt dries the tablecloth and tastes the wine.

Walt Excuse me.

Basil turns back.

Walt I'm afraid this is corked.

Basil . . . I beg your pardon ?

Walt This wine is corked.

Basil I just uncorked it. Didn't you see me ?

Walt doesn't understand.

Walt What ?

Basil (*showing him the cork on the end of the corkscrew*) Look.

Walt No, no . . .

Basil Yes, yes, my dear fellow I took it out. That's how I got the Cortonne <u>out</u> of the bottle <u>into</u> your glass.

Walt No I didn't mean that. The wine (*pointing to the glass*) is corked. It's reacted with the cork.

Basil I'm sorry ?

Walt The wine has reacted with the cork and gone bad.

Basil Gone bad ? May I . . . ?

Basil takes the glass and tastes it. A pause. He replaces the glass, walks away, turns his back and considers his verdict. He returns.

Basil So you don't want it ?

Walt I'd like a bottle that's not corked.

Basil Right ! Right ! That's cost me hasn't it ? No, it doesn't matter. I'll get another bottle.

*Basil takes the bottle away. On his way out,
he addresses the rest of the room.*

Basil I do hope you're all enjoying your meals.

There is no reaction. Basil stops.

Basil I said I hope you're all enjoying your meals.

There is a bit of nodding.

Basil Oh good. How very nice. (*Moves to exit. He turns at the door and calls to Walt*) Excuse me ! . . . Excuse me ! ! ! Table five !

Walt (*roused from his magazine*) . . Er yes ?

Basil Are you having the mackerel or the lamb ?

Walt . . . The lamb.

Basil Thank you. I'll have another one standing by just in case. (*Exits con brio*).

*Sybil comes in, looks around for Basil and
exits.
Polly enters to take the ladies' orders.
Basil comes back in with a fresh bottle.*

Basil Let's give this one a go then. (*Sees Polly*) Polly, would you get Mr. Hutchison his main course please. (*Fawning*) I do apologise for keeping you waiting, Mr. Hutchison. It will be with you in just a moment.

Sybil looks in again.

Sybil Basil.

Basil Hmmmm ?

But she's gone. He decides to follow her, leaving the new bottle on the sideboard just behind Walt.

In the lobby

Sybil is waiting for Basil. Something has made her happy.

Sybil (*sweetly*) How are you getting along with your hotel inspector ?

Basil . . . Fine. Fine ! (*Makes a gesture "It's all under control" and starts to leave*).

Sybil He sells spoons.

Basil (*coming back*) What ?

Sybil I listened in on his phone call. He works for a cutlery firm. But he specialises in spoons.

Basil You listened in ?

Sybil Yes.

Basil You listened in to a private call of one of our guests ?

Sybil That's right Basil.

Basil . . . The little rat! I'll get him for that.

Sybil Now, Basil . . .

Basil Trying that on with me.

Sybil Trying <u>what</u> on?

Basil Pretending he's a hotel inspector, . . . "Can we reserve a channel?", "fresh peas", "ice buckets" . . .

He starts menacingly towards the dining room.

Sybil Basil, it was <u>your</u> mistake. You can't . . .

Basil You let me handle this!

Sybil Basil!!

Basil jumps.

Sybil (*scolding him*) This whole inspector business was in your own imagination. It's nothing to do with him. There's no excuse for rudeness.

Basil is thinking . . .   revenge.

Sybil Do you understand? . . . <u>Do</u> <u>you</u> <u>understand</u>?"

Basil <u>Yes</u>!!

Sybil turns and walks away.

In the dining room

Basil enters and stalks the sitting Hutchison.

Major Papers arrived yet Fawlty ?

Basil Not yet, Major.

He settles behind Hutchison. There is a long pause.

Basil (*quietly*) Spoons, eh ?

Hutchison I'm sorry ?

Basil Spppppppoooons !

Hutchison I beg your pardon ?

Basil I understand you're in the spoon trade.

Hutchison Oh ! Yes . . .

Basil Fascinating. Fascinating. How stimulating for you.

Hutchison Yes, as a matter of . . .

Basil (*savagely*) So much more interesting than being a <u>hotel inspector</u>.

He leaves abruptly. Hutchison is puzzled.
Polly arrives and places an omelette in
front of him.

Hutchison Oh thank you (*looks at it*) Oh ! Miss !

Polly (*turning back*) Yes ?

Hutchison I didn't order this.

Basil (*from afar*) Is there something we can get for you, Mr. Hutchison?
A tea cosy for your pepper pot perhaps?

Hutchison No, no. (*To Polly*) I changed my order.

Basil arrives, spoiling for a fight.

Basil What seems to be the trouble?

Polly Well I thought Mr. Hutchison ordered an omelette, but . . .

Basil He went off it, so we changed it Polly, it's perfectly simple.

Polly I'm sorry but I wasn't told.

Basil I told the chef, so he should have told you.

Polly Well he didn't.

Basil Well is that my fault?

Polly No, is it mine?

Hutchison (*inserting his oar*) No, it's his fault.

Basil What?

Hutchison It's the chef's fault.

There is an ominous pause.

Basil What?

Hutchison Well clearly in a case like this where the order has been
changed and the chef told, it's obviously his respons . . .

Basil You want to run the place?

Hutchison What?

Basil You want to come and run the hotel? Right! Polly! Mr. Hutchison is taking over so I'm having his omelette. (*Trying to get Mr. Hutchison to his feet*) I'm sure with his wide experience and natural charm there'll be no more problems.

Hutchison No, no . . .

Basil Come on then you can't sit about all day, there's lots to be done. (*Jiggling Hutchison's chair to get him up*) Come on!

Sybil (*who has appeared from nowhere*) What is going on, Basil?

Basil (*improvising*) Hello, dear!

Sybil Well?

Basil (*jiggling the chair very slightly*) Is that better?

Hutchison What?

Basil Is that better Mr. Hutchison? Oh good. Well, that's sorted out then.

Sybil is suspicious.

Sybil Is there something wrong?

Hutchison Er . . . yes . . . I have been given an erroneous dish.

Sybil Thank you, Basil, I'll deal with this.

Basil walks innocently away.

Sybil Now, Mr. Hutchison.

Hutchison Well I ordered an omelette but then I changed it.

Sybil I see. I'll just go in the kitchen and find out what's happened.

She heads for the kitchen. Meanwhile Basil is looking at the sideboard. The bottle has gone. He looks around and sees Manuel.

Basil Manuel!

Manuel (*running up*) Si?

Basil (*indicating sideboard*) The bottle.

Manuel Yes!

Basil Where is it?

Manuel Que?

Basil Er . . . donde es . . . ?

Manuel I take it.

Basil groans. Manuel indicates the kitchen.

Manuel I take it, I take it.

Basil (*beckoning gently*) Here.

Manuel Please ?

*Basil takes a soup spoon from the bowl
Manuel is carrying.*

Basil You're a waste of space.

*Basil hustles Manuel off to the kitchen,
passing Sybil en route. She has brought
some paté for Hutchison.*

Sybil There we are, Mr. Hutchison.

Hutchison No, no, no !

Sybil Yes ?

Hutchison I didn't order this.

Sybil You didn't ?

Hutchison No I did not.

Sybil I'm sorry there's an order for a paté for this table.

Hutchison Oh dear me, things are going wrong aren't they ! !

*Basil, coming back with another bottle, is
eavesdropping.*

Basil Hallo Sybil, taking care of it are
you ?

Sybil Yes thank you Basil.

Basil Everything all right then, Mr. Hutchison ?

Hutchison Well it appears that . . .

Sybil We're just sorting it out thank you Basil.

Basil You didn't order the paté maison did you Mr. Hutchison ?

Hutchison No, no, I ordered . . .

Basil Well I'll leave you to deal with it dear.

*Basil walks on well satisfied, removes a
corkscrew from the sideboard, takes a
position behind Walt and starts uncorking
the bottle. The cork comes out, he steps
forward and is about to pour a sample into
Walt's glass when he sees another bottle
open on the table.*

Basil pauses to review his sense-data.

Basil How did you do that?

Walt What?

Basil (*indicating Walt's bottle*) Where did you get it?

Walt . . . Where did I get it?

Basil That's right! How did you get it?

Walt The waiter opened it for me.

Basil The waiter opened it for you!!??

Walt . . . Yes!

*Manuel arrives with Walt's paté. He is
unaware of recent developments.*

Basil I've told you about him haven't I? Oh, never mind!

Manuel leaves, Basil starts to give chase.

Hutchison No, no, no!!

*Polly has just delivered a lamb casserole.
Basil runs across the room.*

Basil (*wildly*) What is it, what is it?!!

Hutchison I didn't order a lamb casserole!

Basil No, no, you didn't, that's right.
He didn't order one Polly so why . . . has . . . he . . . got . . . one?

Polly Because Mrs. Fawlty told me to give him one.

Basil I know how she feels.

Polly There's an order for one for this table.

Basil Who took the order ?

Polly (*valiantly*) . . . I don't know.

Basil . . . Manuel !

Hutchison How can it be so difficult to get a cheese salad ?

Basil . . . You want to run the hotel ?

Hutchison No, no, I . . .

Basil Well shut up then.

Hutchison I beg your pardon ? !

Polly I'll get you a cheese salad, Mr. Hutchison.

Basil (*to Polly*) And don't listen to anyone . . . just get a cheese salad.

Manuel appears.

Manuel Si ?

Basil hits him. He retires.

Hutchison Excuse me ! ! I'm going to change my mind.

Hutchison (*rising*) . . . I won't have the cheese salad. I wish to cancel it. I am not used to being spoken to like that Mr. Fawlty and I have no wish to continue my luncheon.

Basil realises he went a bridge too far.

Basil I do apologise if what I said just now seemed a little . . . brusque.

Hutchison Brusque ? It was <u>rude</u>, Mr. Fawlty.

Basil is astounded.

Hutchison I said . . . <u>rude</u> !

Basil Well I'm deeply sorry if it came over like that. Nothing could have been further from my mind . . .

Hutchison You told me to shut up.

Polly (*brilliantly*) No, no. He told <u>me</u> to shut up.

Hutchison (*to Polly*) What ? He said it to me.

Basil Ah. I was looking at you but I was talking to her. (*Still looking at Hutchison*) Wasn't I, Polly ?

Polly (*straight to Hutchison*) Oh, yes.

Basil (*still to Hutchison*) Ah ! Did you notice then . . . that I was talking to Polly but looking at you ?

Hutchison What ?

Polly (*looking at Basil*) You see, he was looking at you but talking to me. (*To Hutchison*) Wasn't he ?

Basil (*to Polly*) Wasn't I ?

Hutchison (*not sure where to look*) What ?

Polly (*to Hutchison*) So you weren't being rude to him were you Mr. Fawlty ?

Basil (*to Polly*) Absolutely not. You see ?

Hutchison (*to Basil*) . . . Me ?

Basil (*to Hutchison*) Yes.

Hutchison (*to Basil*) Well if you say shut up to someone that's the one you mean to shut up isn't it ?

Polly (*to Basil*) Not necessarily.

Basil (*to Hutchison*) . . . I'm sorry, were you talking to me ?

Hutchison (*to Basil*) Yes.

Polly (*to Basil*) I beg your pardon.

Pause. Hutchison has been successfully confused.

Basil (*to Hutchison*) There ! You see how easily these misunderstandings can occur.

Hutchison Er . . . yes.

Basil So . . . a cheese salad then please Polly.

Polly (*to Basil*) Certainly Mr. Hutchison (*leaves*).

Basil And if there's anything else please don't hesitate to ask.

Hutchison (*after looking around for a moment to see if he is being addressed*) Oh, yes.

Basil makes his way across the room. Manuel creeps past to get Walt's empty plate. He removes it stealthily.

Walt Aaaah !

Basil (*to Manuel*) What are you doing ? (*To Walt*) I'm so sorry. He's from Barcelona. Was the paté to your satisfaction ?

Walt Yes, yes thank you.

Basil Oh good. The chef buys it himself you know.

Walt Buys it ?

Basil Oh, insists on it. I imagine the Cortonne complemented it delightfully.

Walt Yes. It's very good.

Basil Excellent.

Walt More like a '66 really.

Basil Is it ?

Walt . . . Well, a lot more body.

Basil picks up the bottle and expertly judges it's weight.

Basil Quite right. It's always a pleasure to find someone who appreciates the boudoir of the grape. I'm afraid most of the people we get here don't know a Bordeaux from a claret.

Walt . . . A Bordeaux <u>is</u> a claret.

Basil Oh, a <u>Bordeaux</u> is a claret. But <u>they</u> wouldn't know that. You obviously drink a lot.

Basil Wine I mean. Well I don't mean a lot, not too much, a fair amount, the right amount for a connoisseur I mean, that doesn't mean you're ... does it, I mean some people put it away by the crate but that's not being a connoisseur, that's just plain sloshed. Oh, a Bordeaux's one of the clarets all right.

Walt One ?

Basil (*swiftly*) You're down here on business are you ?

Walt receives his casserole from Manuel.

Walt (*dismissively*) Yes.

Basil You're not in the wine trade by any chance ?

Walt No we're not.

Basil We're ?

Walt (*anxious to start on his casserole*) ... I am down here on business with two colleagues and we are not in the wine trade.

Basil Ah, it's just that you're obviously so expert.

Walt ... I am not expert.

Basil Oh you are.

Walt I'm not.

Basil seizes Walt.

Basil Two of them ?

Walt (*astonished*) What ! ?

Basil Two ? . . . <u>Two</u> of them ?

Walt Yes, two of them . . . There are three of us.

Basil is stunned.

Walt . . . They're not with me, they're staying at another . . .

Basil (*recovering his wits*) Quite ! So . . . it's all alright is it ?

Walt . . . What ?

Basil Oh, things in general . . .

Walt Yes.

Basil The wine's really good ?

Walt Yes.

Basil And the paté was alright ?

Walt Yes, I said so.

Basil And the casserole ?

Walt I haven't tasted it <u>yet</u>.

Basil leans forward, sniffs admiringly and smacks his lips.

Basil Mmmmm !

But at this moment, there is an explosion of noise from the vicinity of Hutchison's table.

Basil (*hardly batting an eyelid*) Well I'll leave you to your meal if I may . . . bon appetite.

He hurtles towards Hutchison.

Hutchison (*fortissimo*) This is quite absurd, no I'm sorry but I have had enough of this.

Manuel is pressing Hutchison to accept an omelette.

Hutchison No, no, I don't want it.

Manuel Is very nice.

Hutchison I don't want the bloody thing. I've sent it away once.

Basil whizzes up.

Basil Give it to me.

Hutchison I fail to see how this can possibly happen!

Basil calmly tears up the omelette.

Basil There. I've torn it up. You'll never see it again.

He deposits the remains on the Major's table.
The Major gratefully tucks in. Hutchison continues at the top of his voice.

Hutchison I told you I wanted a cheese salad . . .

Polly arrives with it.

Basil Thank you Polly, there you are sir, one cheese salad, I do hope everything is to your satisfaction.

Hutchison No it is not. It's absolutely ridiculous. I mean you're <u>supposed</u> to be running a <u>hotel</u>!

Basil (*admiring the salad*) My, that does look good.

Hutchison I've been given an omelette, some paté . . .

Basil Look at that cheddar. Delicious!

Hutchison . . . plate of stew then the bloody omelette again ! ! !

Basil (*flashing a quick smile in Walt's direction*) Could we keep it down a little ?

Hutchison I mean I only ordered a cheese salad. It wasn't an elephant's ear on a bun !

Basil Thank you, thank you so much.

Hutchison I've never seen anything like it . . .

Basil Please be quiet.

Hutchison . . . in my life. (*Rising*). Why can't you organize this place efficiently ?

Basil (*pushing him back into his chair*) Well I'm delighted we've sorted it all out now.

Hutchison (*crescendo*) It's not just the service !

Basil Please !

Hutchison You can't get hot water, the vegetables aren't fresh, it takes an hour to . . .

Basil gets his hand across Hutchison's mouth laughing genially at the other guests.

Basil Well I'm glad everything's to your satisfaction now . . .

Hutchison (*very muffled*) It isn't, let me go . . .

Basil Is there anything else <u>at all</u> I can get you, sir ?

Hutchison (*wriggling*) Let me go, I can't breathe.

Basil (*merrily*) Ha ha ha ha ha ha ! (*Hissing*) Shut up then.

Hutchison I can't breathe.

Basil (*prepared to do a deal*) Shut up and I'll let go.

Hutchison (*terribly muffled*) You told me to shut up again !

Basil Look at that <u>lovely</u> cheese !

Hutchison starts threshing about in search of oxygen.

    Basil Stop it.

Basil tightens his grip.

    Basil (*to the room, reassuringly*) It's all right, he's only choking.

Hutchison leaps convulsively. Basil thumps him on the back.

    Basil Don't worry . . . bit of cheese went the wrong way.

More convulsions and thumping. Basil beams, and slips in a quick rabbit punch.
Hutchison goes quiet.

Basil Ah, never mind, he's fainted poor chap!

Basil (*to Walt*) Bit of cheese!

Major Yes please.

In the lobby

Sybil What's happened ?

Basil He's fainted darling.

Sybil Fainted ?

Basil . . . Got a bit of cheese stuck.

They carry Hutchison into the bar.

In the bar

They lay Hutchison down. Sybil arrives.

Sybil . . . Basil you don't faint from getting a bit of cheese stuck.

Basil Well I was giving him a bit of a pat and he sort of . . . moved.

Sybil . . . . . . What have you done, Basil ?

Basil Nothing, he just moved as I . . .

Sybil Oh my God ! Call the doctor.

Basil I am taking care of this, Sybil.

Sybil Call the doctor !

Basil I can handle it ! !

Sybil Call the doctor ! !

Basil Look I can handle it, right ? ! ! !

Sybil looks steadily at Basil.

Basil Right, I'll call the doctor. Obviously, I can't handle it.

He leaves for reception.

At reception

Basil enters, muttering.

Basil I'm just a stupid great sabre-toothed tart so we'll do it my husband's way. (*He picks up the phone, but sees Walt emerging from the dining room*). Ah ! . . . I'm sorry I had to leave you, I trust you enjoyed your lunch ?

Walt (*peremptorily*) Yes, yes, thank you. I was wondering . . .,

Basil The casserole was really good, was it ?

Walt . . . Well it was adequate.

Basil Exactly ! I'm afraid the chef at lunch today is <u>not</u> our regular, but . . .

Basil (*confidentially*) Incidentally, I'm sorry about that fellow choking himself like that.

Walt Yes, is there a telephone I can use ?

Basil Oh please ! Do use this one. (*Hands him receiver*) I don't know <u>how</u> he did it. Ah ! here he comes. Good.

Basil Ah, Mr. Hutchison! There you are . . . What an awful shame about that piece of cheese getting jammed in the old windpipe like that. (*Indicating bar*) Would you like to go in there and discuss it?

Hutchison comes behind the counter.

Hutchison No I'll come in here and discuss it.

Basil . . . (*retreating*) Good idea, I'm sorry it's such a mess.

Hutchison hits him

Basil disappears below the desk. After a pause, he stands up again and smiles warmly at Hutchison.

Basil Well that lie-down obviously did you some good.

Hutchison hits him again and Basil reels towards Walt's end of the desk. Hutchison hits him twice more.

Basil (*to Walt*) Sorry about this.

Hutchison hits him three times more.

He flops out of sight. A pause

> **Hutchison** I am not a violent man, Mr. Fawlty.

> **Basil's voice** Yes you are.

Hutchison But when I am insulted and then attacked I would rather rely on my own mettle than call the police.

Basil's voice Would you ? Would you really ?

Hutchison Stand up like a man.

Basil's voice . . . Bit of trouble with the old leg actually.

Hutchison Come on !

He picks Basil up. Basil has found a stapler.
He shows it to Walt.

> **Basil** Look what I've found !

Hutchison I hope I've made my point.

Basil Oh absolutely ! (*To Walt*) Been looking for that.

Hutchison So let me just add that your hotel is inefficient and badly run, and that you are an extremely <u>rude</u> and <u>discourteous</u> man.

Basil (*happily*) Ah ha ha ha ha.

Hutchison . . . Did I say something funny, Mr. Fawlty ?

Basil . . . Well sort of <u>pithy</u> I suppose.

Hutchison Well here's the punch line.

He hits Basil who falls out of sight.

Hutchison I shall now fetch my belongings and leave. I do not expect to receive a bill.

Hutchison walks off towards the stairs.
Sybil comes in from the bar

Sybil Well you've handled that then, have you?

Basil's voice Yes dear, thank you, leave it to me.

Walt finishes his call and rings off.
Basil hauls himself into view.

Basil Incidentally, I don't know if you realise, he's a regular customer of ours . . . loves it here, it's his second home really but . . .

. . . but we always have to have this little . . . don't know why really, but he seems to like it . . .

Walt Really?

Basil (*pressing on*) There's always the danger though, that somebody's going to think he isn't satisfied about something or that the fighting's real and tell people, you won't mention it will you? I mean, we'd be delighted to give you dinner here tonight to show our gratitude.

Walt ... What?

Basil Dinner tonight. Would you ... ?

Walt (*puzzled*) No I can't tonight, thank you though.

Basil (*desperately*) Tomorrow night?

Walt ... I'm leaving tomorrow. Sorry.

Walt starts to leave.

Basil ... Alright. Fifty pounds then!!!

Walt I'm sorry?

Basil Fifty pounds not to mention it.

Walt Fifty pounds?!!

Basil ... All right, sixty then ... Not to write about it ... you know, letters, books, articles, (*taking out his wallet*).

Walt (*withdrawing nonplussed*) . . . No, no really I don't . . .

Basil runs round the counter and clutches him.

Basil Please! Oh please! We've built this place up for twelve years. If you put this in the book we're finished.

Walt . . . What book?

Basil The hotel guide. Oh . . . I'm sorry I shouldn't have mentioned it.

He emits a strangled high-pitched whine.

Basil Oh what have I done?

Walt Look, I think you've got me confused with somebody else.

Walt I don't have anything to <u>do</u> with a hotel guide.

Basil sobs uncontrollably.

Walt I sell outboard motors, I'm down here for the Exhibition. Look!

Basil The Exhibition ?

Basil . . . You're not an inspector . . . not on the side or anything ?

Walt No.

Basil (*grabbing him*) Swear to God.

Walt (*protesting*) I don't have anything to do with it.

Basil Thank you, thank you. Thank you so much.

He suddenly freezes. A pause.

Basil Thanks.

He disappears into the kitchen.

*Walt shrugs hopelessly, turns, and leaves
the hotel by the main doors. As he does so,
three men walk into the hotel past him.
Here are the inspectors.*

Inspector One (*reading from some brochure*) Twenty-six rooms,
twelve with private baths.

Inspector One Owner's a Basil Fawlty.

*They ring the bell. At that moment
Hutchison comes down the stairs.*

Manuel scampers up, stopping Hutchison.

Manuel Please, please! Mr. Fawlty
want say adios.

Basil says adios.

Basil Manuel, the cream.

The Major joins in.

Major Papers arrived yet, Fawlty ?

Basil No, not yet Major, no.

Basil shakes the case thoroughly and then tucks it under Hutchison's arm.

Basil Now go away. If you ever come back I shall kill you.

Basil propels Hutchison out of the main door.

Basil Thank you, Manuel.

*He strides triumphantly to the counter, and
smiles expansively at the new arrivals.*

Basil Good afternoon.
And what can I do for
you three gentlemen ?

Basil Aaaagh!!

GOURMET NIGHT

CAST

Basil Fawlty	**John Cleese**
Sybil Fawlty	**Prunella Scales**
Manuel	**Andrew Sachs**
Polly	**Connie Booth**
Andre	**Andre Maranne**
Kurt	**Steve Plytas**
Colonel Hall	**Allan Cuthbertson**
Mrs Hall	**Ann Way**
Mr Twitchen	**Richard Caldicot**
Mrs Twitchen	**Betty Huntley-Wright**
Major Gowen	**Ballard Berkeley**
Miss Tibbs	**Gilly Flower**
Miss Gatsby	**Renee Roberts**
Mr Heath	**Jeffrey Segal**
Mrs Heath	**Elizabeth Benson**
Master Heath	**Tony Page**

In the forecourt of Fawlty Towers

Basil is fiddling under the bonnet of his car. It is clearly a real mother of an old car. He makes a final adjustment and strides round to sit in the driver's seat. He presses the starter, twice, without success.

Basil Oh come on, is it so difficult for you to start?

Basil I mean, it's so <u>basic</u>. If you don't go, there's very little point in having you.

He tries again.

He gives up, gets out and goes round to the front of the car again. He takes a delicious looking savoury from a small pile he has placed on the side of the engine, pops it in his mouth, and starts fiddling again. After a moment he steps back.

Basil Now just pull yourself together.

He returns to the driver's seat and presses the starter. It whines pitifully.

Basil Now look!!

Manuel runs down the steps.

Manuel Mr. Fawlty ! Telephone ! !

Basil Oh . . . where's Sybil ?

Manuel . . . Que ?

Basil Where's . . . Sy . . . bil ?

Manuel . . . Where's the bill ?

Basil No ! No ! I own the place. I don't pay bills. Where's my wife ?

Manuel She not there.

Basil She is there !

Silence.
Manuel looks helpless.

Basil . . . Oh never mind, I'll do it !

He leaps out of the car and strides towards the hotel.

Basil <u>I'll</u> fix the car, <u>I'll</u> answer the telephone, then you can all handcuff and blindfold me and I'll clean the windows . . .

He disappears inside with Manuel scampering after him.

Inside the lobby

Basil steams in. Manuel somehow overtakes him.

> **Manuel** (*indicating receiver lying on reception desk.*) This way please.

> **Basil** I <u>know</u>!

But just before he gets to the telephone, Sybil appears from the office and answers it herself.

> **Sybil** Hallo?

Sybil Oh, André, thank you for calling. We're absolutely delighted with him . . . really, André, he's wonderful . . .

Basil catches Manuel and brings him back.

Basil (*pointing to Sybil*) <u>This</u> . . . Sybil.

Basil <u>This</u> . . . Basil.

Basil <u>This</u> . . .

Basil . . . smack on head.

Manuel slinks off. Basil turns back towards the forecourt.

Sybil Just one moment André . . . Basil!

Basil (*halting*) Yes dear?

Sybil . . . Have you taken the car in yet?

Basil I'm just dealing with it dear.

Sybil You're not trying to do it yourself are you Basil?

Basil discovers a change of subject on the wall.

Basil Have you seen this mark here?

Sybil Did you hear what I said?

Basil Yes, dear. It's a bit of a scratch . . .

Sybil Take it into the garage Basil.

Basil (*absently*) Yes, yes, just having a look at it dear.

Sybil (*returning to phone*) I'm sorry André, where was I? Oh yes. Well, he's the best chef we've ever had and we can't thank you enough for finding him for us . . .

Basil checks that Sybil is not looking and slips into the kitchen.

Sybil Can you come and have dinner with us on Sunday? . . . Well, there's something we want your advice about . . . oh, lovely, see you then. Goodbye.

Sybil rings off and walks towards the kitchen. As she does so, Polly comes in through the main entrance.

Sybil Hallo, Polly.

Polly Hallo ! I've sold a sketch ! Can you come and have a drink to celebrate ?

Sybil Really ? I'd love to . . .

They enter the kitchen together.

In the kitchen

In the kitchen Kurt and Manuel are preparing food. Basil is lurking by another pile of delicious savouries.

Polly Hallo.

Kurt and Manuel Hallo.

Sybil (*to Kurt*) Kurt, André can come on Sunday. (*To Basil*) I thought you were taking the car in.

She sees Basil who is quickly popping a savoury into his mouth.

Sybil Are you at those again ?

Basil I've just taken one dear.

Sybil (*taking the plate away from him*) I think you've had enough of those, Basil. Now will you deal with the car, please.

Kurt sees Basil munching as he moves off.

Kurt Good Mr. Fawlty ?

Basil Superb.

Polly (*giving Sybil a glass of wine*) There you are. For you Mr. Fawlty ?

Basil Thank you Polly.

Sybil Are you going to do the car ?

Basil In a moment, my little piranha fish. (*To Polly*) What's all this, then ?

Polly I've sold a sketch.

Basil One of yours ?

Kurt I bought it Mr. Fawlty. She's very talented.

Polly offers Kurt a glass of wine.

Kurt Oh no, Polly, I won't.

Polly Oh come on.

Kurt No thank you.

Polly Oh please. I bought it to thank you.

Kurt No honestly.

Polly Don't you like it ?

Kurt Too much. Really, not when I'm working. You drink it for me Manny.

Manuel accepts gratefully.

Basil (*raising his glass to Polly*) Well . . . Cheerio.

Sybil (*neatly confiscating his glass*) Cheerio Basil.

Basil Well that smelt nice.

Kurt produces the sketch he has bought.

Kurt Here it is Mr. Fawlty.

Basil studies it. It is clearly of the abstract persuasion.

Kurt She's really got something you know Mr. Fawlty.

Basil Has she?

Polly Well worth 50p anyway.

Basil Do you win a bun for guessing what it is?

Polly It's Manuel.

Basil What?

Manuel It's me.

Basil . . . Where?

Kurt Manny's my friend (*putting his arm round Manuel's shoulders*). We're good friends eh?

Manuel Si.

Basil (*handing the sketch back*) Yes, very modern. Very socialist.

Kurt takes it and kisses it warmly.

Basil (*moving off*) Something to remember him by . . . you know, when he leaves.

Sybil You still here Basil?

Basil No. I went a couple of minutes ago. But I expect I'll be back soon (*exits*).

Sybil studies the sketch. Kurt sees Manuel performing some culinary misdeed.

Kurt No, no Manuel!! Look, like this, . . . gently.

He shows Manuel, in the traditional manner of the golf pro guiding the bit of fluff's full swing.

Sybil (*handing Polly the sketch*) I like that. Will you do me one ?

Polly (*rather taken aback*) – Of Manuel ?

Sybil Yes. It'll look nice on Basil's bedside table (*exits*).

Polly (*to Kurt*) Two in a day. That's as many as Van Gogh sold in a lifetime.

Kurt Ah but he didn't have Manny as a model.

In reception

As Polly appears, Sybil is looking out of the main entrance towards the forecourt.

The forecourt of Fawlty Towers

The car draws away. Basil waves friendlily to Sybil, as he disappears down the drive and out of the gate. From the road outside we see the car comes to a halt right round the corner. Basil gets out, takes a handful of savouries out of his pocket, opens up the bonnet and starts peering under it. He is in no way in a garage . . .

In the dining room.
Sunday evening

Basil, Sybil and André are sitting at one of the tables. Some other guests are apparent, including a couple, Xerxes and Yolande Johnson and their eleven-year-old son Ronald. The food at the table looks great and is.

Sybil (*not utterly unhistrionically*) Ohh. Mmmm. This is wonderful.

André I told you, he is one of the best.

Sybil He's almost as good as you André. Oh!! It's absolutely <u>divine</u>, Basil.

Basil It is good isn't it.

Sybil Listen to him. The only place I've ever really seen him eat is your restaurant André, and now he is stuffing it away like a hamster.

Basil Sybil, really.

Sybil We're going to have to buy him a great big wheel to run around in when he's got a moment, or he'll get like a big bad-tempered tomato.

Basil I believe we were discussing the Gourmet Evening, Sybil.

Sybil Do you know André, he burst his zip this morning.

Basil (*in a superior manner*) Oh dear.

Sybil What darling ?

Basil You're embarrassing André

Sybil No dear, I'm embarrassing you. (*She pats Basil's stomach*) Look at that.

Basil Well I'd better see to the guests. Why don't you have another vat of wine dear ?

Basil rises and starts to circulate. The first table he passes is the Major's.

Basil Good evening, Major. Did you enjoy your soup ?

Major Tasted a bit off to me, Fawlty.

Basil Well it was made with <u>fresh</u> mushrooms actually, Major.

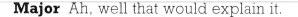

Major Ah, well that would explain it.

*A flicker of olympian despair crosses
Basil's face. He moves on to the Johnson's
table.*

Basil Good evening. Is everything to your satisfaction ?

Xerxes Yes thank . . .

Yolande (*interrupting*) Well . . .

She turns expectantly to their son.

Ronald I don't like the chips.

Basil Sorry ?

Ronald The chips are awful.

Yolande Ronald.

Basil smiles balefully.

Basil Oh dear. What's er . . . what's <u>wrong</u> with them then ?

Ronald They're the wrong shape and they're just awful.

Yolande I'm afraid he gets everything cooked the way he likes it, at home.

Basil Does he, does he ?

Ronald Yes I do, and it's better than this pig's garbage.

Yolande (*slightly amused*) Now Ronald.

Ronald These eggs look like you laid them.

Xerxes (*to Ronald, friendlily*) Now look here old boy . . .

Yolande Shut up !! Leave him alone ! (*She turns to Basil*) He's very clever, rather highly strung.

Basil Yes, yes, he should be.

Ronald fixes Basil contemptuously.

Ronald Haven't you got any <u>proper</u> chips ?

Basil Well these are proper French Fried Potatoes. You see, our chef . . . is Continental.

Ronald Couldn't you get an English one?

Basil is momentarily stumped. Yolande laughs. Basil's eyes move to her.

Yolande But hasn't he got any of the frozen crinkly ones?

Basil I'm afraid he hasn't.

Yolande Oh!?

Ronald Why not!?

Basil Well, he likes cooking. That's why he became a chef.

Yolande (*to Ronald*) Why don't you eat just one or two dear?

Ronald They're the wrong shape.

Basil (*solicitously*) What shape do you usually have? Micky Mouse shape? Smarties shape? Amphibious landing craft shape? Poke in the eye shape?

Ronald . . . God, you're dumb.

Ronald appraises him.

Yolande Oh, now . . .

Basil is holding himself on a very tight rein.

Basil Well is there something you'd like instead, Sonny?

Ronald . . . I'd like some bread and salad cream.

Basil . . . To eat? Well . . . (*he points*) there's the bread, and there's the mayonnaise.

Ronald I said <u>salad</u> <u>cream</u>, stupid.

Basil We <u>don't</u> <u>have</u> salad cream. The chef made <u>this</u> (*indicating mayonnaise*) <u>fresh</u> this morning.

Ronald What a dump!

Xerxes (*offering Ronald the mayonnaise*) This is <u>very</u> <u>good</u>.

Yolande (*to Xerxes, coldly*) He likes salad cream.

Ronald (*to Basil, pointing at the mayonnaise*). That's puke that is.

Basil Well at least it's fresh puke, ha ha!

Yolande (*shocked*) Oh dear!!

Basil (*indignantly*) Well <u>he</u> said it!

Yolande (*loftily*) May I ask why you don't have any proper salad cream. I mean most restaurants . . .

Basil Well <u>our</u> chef only buys it on special occasions, you know, gourmet nights and so on, but . . . <u>when</u> he's got a bottle he's a genius with it. He can unscrew the top like Robert Carrier. It's a treat to watch (*he mimes*).

Basil <u>Right</u> on the plate.

Basil Magic! Mind you, he's highly trained. He's a wizard with a tin-opener too. He got a Pulitzer Prize for that. He has the stuff in a saucepan before you can say 'Haute Cuisine'. You name it, he'll heat it up and scrape it off the pan for you. Mind you, skill like that isn't acquired overnight. Still, I'll get some salad cream, you never know when Henry Kissinger is going to drop in.

Yolande is silenced. Basil smiles charmingly, looks at his watch, and in so doing elbows Ronald in the head.

Basil Sorry, sorry!

Xerxes Nice man.

Meanwhile, Sybil and André are deep in conversation.

André No, no seriously, I think it's a very good idea.

Sybil You really do?

André I promise you, people round here are getting more and more keen on good food.

Basil arrives back at the table and sits down.

Basil Well, so much for tonight's guests. Ignorant rabble.

Sybil Ssssh!

André Oh, there's always a few Mr. Fawlty.

Basil Not on Gourmet Night there won't be. (*Slightly too loudly*) None of these proles.

Sybil Basil!

Basil Tch.

Sybil Now André thinks Thursday nights would be best.

Basil Thursdays?

André I think so.

Basil Right. And on the other nights we'll just have a big trough of baked beans and garnish it with a couple of dead dogs.

Sybil Well that's settled them.

André Good. And I'm pleased for Kurt too, it'll be good for him to have something special to do . . . I'd like a word with him, do you mind?

Sybil Of course not.

André rises, and goes towards the kitchen.

Basil I'll get the menus printed tomorrow.

Sybil Polly can do the menus.

Basil No she can't.

Sybil Yes she <u>can</u>. <u>You</u> can do the advertisement. But don't get all toffee-nosed.

Basil I just want to keep the riff-raff out, Sybil.

In the kitchen

André and Kurt are talking. Manuel is busying himself.

André Well good luck my old friend, it's good to have you down here.

Kurt Thank you for . . . well, you know.

André Forget it . . . nice to have met you, Manuel.

Kurt (*putting an arm round Manuel*) He's my friend.

Manuel One night I cook you both Paella.

They all laugh. André turns to leave.

André And Kurt . . .

Kurt looks at him. André waves a humorous admonishing finger.

Kurt . . . You don't trust me ?

André Ciao.

André goes back into the dining room.

Kurt (*grandiloquently*). Manuel! <u>Together</u>, you and I make Fawlty Towers <u>famous</u> for its cooking!

Manuel Como?

Kurt . . . Oh you're so <u>cute</u>.

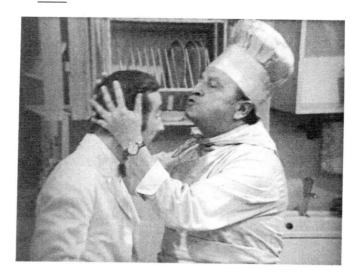

In the dining room.   Gourmet Night

A hand-painted Polly-style menu prominently displays the message 'Gourmet Night At Fawlty Towers'. Basil, in evening dress is meticulously adjusting cutlery on one of the tables. Picks up one spoon and looks at it.

Basil Manuel!

He gives the spoon to Manuel. Manuel takes it, breathes heavily on it, wipes it on his jacket, and puts it back in its place. Basil picks it up and gives it to him again.

Basil No, no, get a <u>clean</u> one.

Manuel Is clean now.

Basil Is dirty now.

Manuel runs off with it. Basil now picks up a menu, and regards it with disapproval. Polly comes in, and places a single flower on the table. She glances at Basil.

Polly Do you like the menu ?

Basil No I don't.

Polly (*happily*) Oh good.

Basil . . . What ?

Polly Thank you. Thank you so much.

She exits, passing Manuel, who is coming in with a new spoon. He is about to put it down when Basil sees him.

Basil No, no, give it to me.

Basil takes it and puts it in place. They both look at it. Basil re-adjusts it. They look again. Cautiously, Manuel inches towards it and reaches out. Basil smacks his hand. Sybil enters from the lobby.

Sybil Well Basil, guess who's just rung up to cancel at twelve minutes past seven ?

Basil . . . Who ?

Sybil The Coosters.

Basil What ?! All <u>four</u> ?

Sybil Marvellous, isn't it.

Basil Tch. What did they say ?

Sybil One of them's ill.

Basil Well let's hope it's nothing trivial.

There is a pause. Basil busies himself.

Sybil You realise there are <u>four</u> <u>people</u> at our grand opening dinner ?.

Basil Never mind !

Sybil Never mind ? There's four people, Basil. Shall we feed them in the kitchen ?

Basil (*exhortingly*) Look who they <u>are</u> dear ! Colonel and Mrs. Hall, <u>both</u> J.P.'s, and Leslie Twitchen, one of Torquay's <u>leading</u> Rotarians.

Sybil Oh, that'll put us on the map.

Basil He's this year's treasurer, Sybil.

Sybil I should never have let you write the advert. Fancy putting 'No riff-raff'.

Sybil exits briskly.

Basil (*calling after her*). When you're presenting haute cuisine, Sybil, you don't want the working classes sticking their nose in it.

Basil puts his head into the kitchen.

In the kitchen

Polly is preparing some food.

Basil Everything all right ? Where's Kurt ?

Polly He's getting some wine from the cellar, with Manuel.

In the dining room

Basil comes back into the room, looks round proudly and rubs his hands together

Basil Ah, this is what it's all about.

The two old ladies peer in from the lobby, and look around. Basil sees them.

Basil Now you two ! You're supposed to be in your rooms.

Miss Gatsby Oh !

Basil You're not allowed down here tonight, remember ?

Miss Gatsby Doesn't it look pretty !

Miss Tibbs What are you cooking ?

Basil I'll send you up a menu with your cheese and biscuits. Now skit.

As he shoos them out, Sybil appears
behind them.

Sybil They're here Basil.

Basil What ?

Sybil The Halls are here !

Basil gasps. Sybil hurries off.

Miss Gatsby and Miss Tibbs The Halls !

The ladies bustle off. Basil straightens his
tie, and takes a deep breath. Manuel runs
in from the kitchen.

Manuel Mr. Fawlty please. I very
upset.

Basil Not now Manuel. Later.

Basil strides out leaving Manuel flapping.

In the bar

*The Halls are talking to Sybil. Mrs. Hall is
extremely small. Colonel Hall has a
commanding manner and a facial twitch.*

Colonel When I went out for my stroll this morning, I thought it was
going to be rather warm (*he twitches*) but in the event it turned out
quite cool and then it started to cloud over after lunch, contrary of
course to what the forecast said (*he twitches*) and it won't surprise me
if we get a little rain tonight.

Sybil Still it's been a lovely summer hasn't it?

Basil strides in.

Basil Ah Colonel! How delightful to
see you again.

The Colonel turns round.

Colonel .... Sorry!?

Basil How delightful to see you again. We met last year at the Golf
Club dinner dance, you may remember?

A pause.

Colonel No I don't.

Basil Fine, we didn't talk for long, just good evening really, a blink of the eye and you'd have missed it. As indeed you did, most understandably.

The Colonel twitches. Basil stares, puzzled.

Basil Sorry?

Colonel . . . What?

Sybil nudges Basil.

Basil Oh I'd forgotten! Well, hasn't it been unremarkable.

Colonel . . . What?

Basil The <u>weather</u> . . . I was just thinking how unremarkable it's been really. Ha! Hardly worth talking about. . . in fact <u>not</u> worth talking about. Only a fool would, ha, ha, ha!

Sybil nudges him. Basil looks at her and senses he should change the subject.

Basil And how is that <u>lovely</u> daughter of yours?

Sybil (*quietly*) Dead.

Basil grabs the Colonel's lapel and examines the material keenly.

Basil I like your suit. Isn't it lovely. The way those stripes go up and down, really super. How much did that cost then?

The Colonel is irritated.

Colonel . . . Who <u>are</u> you?

Basil stares at the Colonel blankly. The dropping of the death brick is having a paralysing effect.

Colonel . . . I don't know your name.

Basil (*to Sybil under his breath*)
What is it ?

Sybil What ?

Basil (*in a frenzied whisper*) My name.

Sybil (*calmly*) This is my husband, Basil Fawlty.

Basil That's it ! !

Colonel What ?

Basil I was just. . . off. . . very odd. . . how do you do ?

*He offers his hand. The Colonel shakes it
and twitches.*

Basil May I introduce my wife ?

Colonel She just introduced you.

Basil What a coincidence !

Colonel Yes I don't think you know my wife. . .

He turns towards Mrs. Hall.

Basil (*to Sybil*) Dead ?

Sybil nods.

Colonel May I introduce Mrs. Hall ?

Basil Oh hallo! Didn't see you there.
Don't get up.

*Sybil nudges him. Basil takes another look
at Mrs. Hall.*

Basil Oh!

Sybil What would you like to drink, Mrs. Small? <u>Hall</u>!

Basil Yes! What would you like? A short or . . . oh!

Sybil A sherry, perhaps, would you like a sherry?

Mrs. Hall That would be very nice.

Basil Oh good. Large or . . . or
. . . <u>not</u> quite so large?

Colonel Two, small and dry.

Basil Oh . . . I don't know.

Colonel What ?

Basil I wouldn't say that.

Colonel (*irritably*) Two small, dry, sherries.

Basil Oh I see what you mean !

The Colonel twitches. The bell at reception sounds. Basil bows and withdraws.

Sybil Would you like to sit over here ?

She ushers the Halls to a suitable table.

In the lobby

Mr. and Mrs. Twitchen are waiting by reception. Basil sails up.

Basil Ah good evening. Welcome to Fawlty Towers.

Mr. Twitchen Good evening.

Basil (*sveltely*) How very au fait of you to come to our little culinary soirée this evening.

Mrs. Twitchen We always like to support any new venture in Torquay Mr. Fawlty.

Mr. Twitchen It's such an unusual idea. I do hope it works out.

Basil Well we have our hopes.

Polly appears from the kitchen. She looks rather agitated.

Polly Mr. Fawlty!

Basil Ah Polly! Would you take Mrs. Twitchen's coat please?

Polly Yes of course.

She starts helping Mrs. Twitchen out of her coat.

Basil (*with a courtly gesture towards the bar*) Would you care . . . ?

Mr. Twitchen moves in the direction indicated but halts. He has noticed that the coat-removing is not going well. Polly clearly has her mind on other things.

Polly Mr. Fawlty.

Basil Yes?

Polly Can I have a word with you?

Basil Yes.

A pause.

Basil (*to the Twitchens*) This is Polly, who'll be serving you tonight.

They smile at her.

Polly Er . . .

Basil Well?

Polly It's Kurt.

Basil Yes?

Polly He's potted . . . the shrimps.

Basil What?

Polly He's <u>potted</u> . . . the shrimps.

Basil . . . Shrimps ? We're not having shrimps, Polly . . .

Another pause. The Twitchens look at Polly a little oddly. Basil indicates the bar and they all move off towards it. Polly darts after them and taps Basil's arm. They all stop.

Polly (*meaningfully*) He's <u>soused</u> . . . the herrings.

Basil What are you on about ? !

Polly (*slowly*) He's <u>pickled</u> . . . the onions and he's <u>smashed</u> the eggs <u>in</u> <u>his</u> <u>cups</u>, <u>under</u> <u>the</u> <u>table</u> (*she rolls her eyes strangely*).

Basil (*to the Twitchens*) Excuse me. (*To Polly sotto voce*) Have you been drinking Polly ?

Polly No, not me !

Basil (*hissing*) Well, will you behave yourself !

He turns to the Twitchens

Basil I'm so sorry to have kept you.

As they lead off into the bar, Polly pecks at his sleeve imploringly.

Polly Please.

The Twitchens have seen this.

Basil Bit of cotton.

He flicks it imperiously away and gestures grandly towards the bar.

Basil Now may I offer you a little aperitif, while you decide what you would like for dinner ?

They move off towards the bar and this time Polly lets them go.

Mr. Twitchen Oh thank you. Lotte ?

Mrs. Twitchen Tomato juice, please, dear.

Mr. Twitchen And for me.

They enter the bar.

In the bar

Sybil is behind the bar, pouring the sherries. Basil calls to her.

Basil Two tomato juices! Ah Colonel!

He hastens ahead to make the introductions.

Basil Colonel and Mrs. Hall, may I introduce Mr. and Mrs. Tw....

A pause.

Basil Have you met?

Colonel No we haven't.

Basil (*to Mr. Twitchen*) Have you?

Mr. Twitchen No.

Basil Oh, good. Well what would you like to drink?

Mrs. Hall What?

Basil To drink?

Mrs. Hall I didn't catch the name.

Basil You didn't catch it? What a rotten bit of luck!

Colonel Well?

Basil Fine, thanks.

Colonel No, we <u>still</u> don't know the <u>name</u>.

Basil Fawlty. Basil Fawlty.

Colonel No, <u>theirs</u>.

Basil Oh, <u>theirs</u>! Oh I see, of course, I thought you meant mine. My, it's warm in here! I could do with a drink too. Another sherry?

Colonel Well, <u>are</u> you going to introduce us?

Basil Didn't I? Of course. (*He looks at his watch*) Good Lord! Is that the time? I didn't realise.

Basil (*in a businesslike manner*) May I present Mr. and Mrs? Now . . .

Colonel What?!!!

Basil (*patiently*) . . . Mr. and Mrs. . . .

Basil lets out a little cry and faints backwards.
He lies still for a couple of seconds, opens his eyes and looks up.

Basil Sorry! I fainted.
Now, I'll get your tomato juices.

He rises.

Basil Ah, I feel better for that.

He heads for the bar.

Mr. Twitchen (*to the Halls*) The name's Twitchen.

Colonel Hall. How do you do. Would you care to join us?

They all sit down at the Halls' table. Sybil comes up
with drinks and more Gourmet Night menus.

Sybil Here are your tomato juices.

She puts them down.

Mr. Twitchen Thank you.

Sybil Would you like to see the menus?

Colonel Ah, good.

Sybil distributes them.

Sybil A menu for you, madam . . . here we are. And for you sir.

They read the menus keenly.

Mrs. Hall Lobster thermidor!

Mrs. Twitchen What are Tournedos Medici?

Sybil Well, they're done in a port and cream sauce . . .

At the bar

Basil is recovering and pouring out some more sherries. Polly appears at his elbow.

Polly (*quietly*) Mr. Fawlty.

Basil Yes ? What do you want ?

Polly Please put the bottle down.

Basil What <u>is</u> it ?

Polly Please put the <u>bottle</u> down.

Basil (*impatiently*) What do you <u>want</u> ? !

Polly . . . Kurt is drunk.

Basil (*very calm*) . . . I see.

He drops the bottle. It smashes. The guests jump.

Basil (*calling*) Sorry ! (*To Polly*) Drunk ? !

Polly Almost unconscious.

Basil makes a supreme effort of self control. He fails.

Basil Sorry!!

Basil (*to Polly*) . . . How?

Polly I'm not sure. It happened so quickly. He had a row with Manuel.

Basil Manuel?

Polly . . . He's got a crush on him.

Basil A <u>what</u>?

Polly A crush . . . you know . . . in love . . .

A pause. Then, in despair, Basil hits the bar counter with his fist. Unfortunately, he catches a light metal tray, which spins in the air and lands loudly. The guests jump a lot.

Basil (*to the guests*) Sorry!! Sorry. Excuse me!

Basil steams round the bar past Polly. She pursues him into the lobby.

In the lobby

Basil I knew it. I knew this would happen if I hired a Frenchman.

Polly He's Greek Mr. Fawlty.

Basil Greek?

Polly Of course.

Basil Well that's worse. They invented it.

He opens the kitchen door.

In the kitchen

Kurt is standing very unsteadily against the wall with a bottle in his hand. Basil walks up to him.

> **Basil** (*calmly but with great authority*) Give that to me Kurt. Come on.

Kurt mumbles and holds the bottle away from Basil.

> **Basil** (*firmly*) Give that bottle to me.

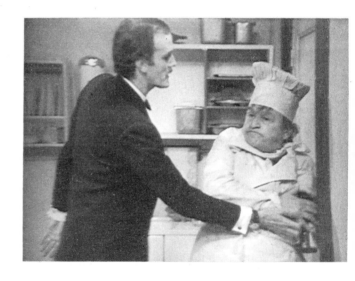

> **Kurt** No. Leave me alone.

> **Basil** (*patiently*) Give it to me.

He reaches for the bottle but Kurt resists.

Basil Now, look . . .

Kurt Manuel. He doesn't love me!

Basil Well you must give these things time.

Kurt I want Manuel!!

Basil Well I'm sure we can
arrange something.

Basil Now can I have the bottle?

Kurt Oh he's so sweet.

Basil Yes, he is.

Kurt He's wonderful.

Basil I know.

*Basil grabs at the bottle. They struggle.
Basil falls backwards, getting his head in a
plate of salmon mousse. He pushes Kurt
away. Kurt staggers back and collapses.
Basil starts slapping his face.*

Basil Kurt! Come on Kurt! (*To Polly*) Get me some black coffee.

Polly He can't drink it. He's out.

Basil We'll bring him round, he's only drunk half a bottle.

Polly We <u>won't</u>, Mr. Fawlty.

Basil looks at the other empties and starts strangling Kurt. Polly tries to restrain him, but he stops only when he hears Manuel's voice calling from behind the doors to the dining room.

Manuel Now, listen! Listen to me, Kurty! I come in now but no cuddle. You hear me? <u>No</u> cuddle.

Manuel pushes the door open cautiously and comes in. Basil grabs him and hustles him over to the heap that is Kurt.

Basil Look what you've done!

Manuel recoils.

Manuel Dead?!

Basil To the world.

Polly He's drunk, Manuel.

Basil (*to Manuel*) This is your fault.

Manuel Que?

190

Basil You only had to be civil to him.

Manuel Seville?

Basil Kind!

Manuel That not enough. You no understand. He want <u>kiss</u> me.

Basil Oh, what's one little kiss!

Polly has been thinking.

Polly Mr. Fawlty!!

Basil Yes?

Polly Why don't you call André and ask him if he can do the cooking?

Basil ... André?! He's <u>open</u> tonight!
He's open on a Thursday you ...
cloth-eared bint.

Polly <u>Yes</u>! But he could cook them <u>there</u>!!

Basil stares at her.

Polly You could get them in the car!

A pause.

Basil (*in purest joy*) Oh!

He grabs Manuel with similar intent. Manuel yelps.

Basil Yech! What am I doing?!

He releases Manuel and stands, poised for thought.

Basil ... Right!!

He runs to the door

Polly (*calling after him*) We've got the starters.

In the cocktail bar

The four guests are genuinely impressed.

Mr. Twitchen Well I've never seen a menu like this in Torquay before.

Mrs. Hall Except at the Imperial.

Mr. Twitchen Oh yes, but not in a smaller place.

Colonel Quite. Most encouraging. Petal and I take our eating pretty seriously, but round here ...

Mrs. Twitchen ... I <u>can't</u> resist the lobster.

Colonel No. Tournedos for me, every time.

Sybil Would you like another drink?

Colonel No, but we're nearly ready to order.

Sybil Certainly. We'll be with you in a moment.

She looks round for Basil.

In reception

Basil is on the phone, in a high state of excitement.

Basil You can't do lobster, yes I see, right, <u>right</u> . . . but André, the <u>tournedos</u>? . . . yes I'm sorry, I'm <u>sorry</u> . . .

Sybil enters from the bar.

Sybil Basil!

Basil Yes, of course I want the duck. Yes, that's marvellous, but <u>can</u> you do a sauce or two? . . . Oh, yes, yes, wonderful! That's it! Thank you, thank you, André.

Basil puts the phone down.

Sybil Why are you talking to André?

Basil What is it, what is it?!

Sybil They're ready to order Basil.

He takes a sheet of paper and inserts it in the typewriter.

Basil Stall them, stall them!

Sybil What!?

Basil Stall them!! Stall them, you stupid woman!! Tell them some lie.

He starts typing furiously with two fingers.
One is off form.

Sybil (*firmly*) What is going on?

Basil Sssh!!

Sybil Will you just tell me what you're doing?!

The keys have jammed.

Basil We've got to change the menu.

He unjams them and types on, midst a flurry of oaths.

Sybil Why?... Why?... <u>Why</u>!!!!????

Basil spins round at her.

Basil (*frantically*) Listen, he's in there, he's out, flat out, so André's...

Sybil Who is?

Basil ...What?

Sybil Who is out?

Basil Kurt. Kurt! Who d'you think, Henry Kissinger?

He attacks the typewriter again.

Sybil What do you mean 'out'?

Basil He's drunk.

Sybil ...Drunk?

Basil Inebriated! Soused! Potted! Got it?

Sybil is stunned.

Sybil . . . I don't believe it.

Basil I don't either. Perhaps it's a dream.

He stops and bangs his head on the desk.

Nothing happens.

Basil No, it's not a dream, we're stuck with it.

He pulls the sheet out of the typewriter.

Basil So André's doing the cooking and I'll collect it in the car.

Sybil What's he cooking?

Basil Duck.

Sybil . . . Duck?

Basil <u>Duck</u>!

Sybil . . . <u>Duck</u>!?

Basil Yes, <u>duck</u>!!!! You know . . .

He runs around flapping his arms up and down and quacking.

In the bar

Basil flies in, attracting some attention.

Effortlessly he slips into his smarmiest 'Mine Host' persona.

Basil I'm so sorry to have kept you all waiting.

Colonel Well, we'd like to order now . . .

Basil Er quite . . . Er . . .

Colonel (*going straight on*) My wife would like the lobster as her main . . .

Basil (*interrupting*) <u>Ah</u>, yes! Er, excuse me . . .

Colonel Yes?

Basil There is one small thing . . . I'm afraid you've been given the wrong menus. This is tonight's menu.

Colonel What?

Basil starts collecting the originals.

Basil I'm sorry, but the chef changed his mind . . . and forgot to tell us. He's like that, brilliant but temperamental.

Colonel What, changed everything?!

Basil I'm afraid so. It wasn't good enough, so he just chucked it away. He's such a perfectionist.

Mr. Twitchen The lobster?

Basil (*stylishly*) Lobster, tournedos, you name it, it's in the bin.

Mr. Twitchen How extraordinary.

Basil Yes. Lucky old bin, I say! So <u>this</u> is your new menu.

He beams at the Colonel. The Colonel starts reading it out.

Colonel Duck with orange . . . duck with cherries . . . duck surprise?

He comes to a full stop.

Mrs. Twitchen . . . What's duck surprise?

Basil That's duck, without orange or cherries.

The Colonel is beginning to bristle.

Colonel Is that all there is, <u>duck</u>?

Basil peers at the menu to check.

Basil . . . Yeeees . . . (*quickly*). Done, of course, the three extremely different ways.

Colonel Well, what do you do, if you don't like duck?

Basil Well, if you don't like duck . . . (*humorously*) you're rather stuck.

He laughs, non-infectiously, but . . .

Mrs. Hall Well, fortunately I love it!

Basil Oh good! So . . . it's four ducks, is it?

Mr. Twitchen . . . Looks like it.

Colonel (*angrily*) Well, isn't there anything <u>else</u>?

Basil (*playing for time*) What?

Colonel (*dangerously*) . . . <u>Apart from the</u> duck.

Basil Not . . . as such.

He leans towards them, lowering his voice confidentially.

Basil To be perfectly frank, the chef has got a bit of a duck craze on at the moment, but I'm glad to say . . . it's on the wane already.

Colonel Well I'd hardly call this a gourmet menu!

Basil . . . Too much duck?

Colonel <u>Of course there's too much duck</u>!!!

Basil reviews the menu, thoughtfully.

Basil Yes, there's an <u>awful</u> lot, isn't there. I'll have to have a word with him about this.

In the kitchen

Sybil is kneeling by Kurt's side, looking for signs of life. She shakes her head. Polly comes up.

Sybil You were right. Now he's getting this duck from André . . .

Polly Yes, I don't know what vegetables he's put on.

Sybil Well, let's find out, at least we can do those.

Basil comes running in, followed by Manuel.

Basil Three salmon mousses for starters. Polly ! And one mullet with mustard sauce, for Mrs. Hall. Where are the mullets ?

Polly There !

Polly points and starts preparing three portions of the mousse.
Basil hurries to a dish containing some mullet, and takes a couple out and starts putting them on a plate. The atmosphere is urgent but co-operative.

Sybil What are you doing about vegetables, Basil ?

Basil Same. Same as on the other menu, dear.

Sybil André's not doing any ?

Basil No, no, do them, you and Polly do them . . .

He pours mustard sauce on to the mullet, and picks up the plate.

Basil While I'm out in the car get them ready, right ?

Basil Ready, Polly?

Polly Yes.

Basil Manuel!

Manuel takes the plate of mullet. Basil indicates the three plates of mousse.

Basil Two for table nine, Polly. Manuel, one of these, and this for table four. Come on.

In the dining room

The Halls and the Twitchens are sitting at separate tables. Polly goes to the Twitchen's table with the mousses and Manuel to the Halls' with his two plates. He puts them down the wrong way round.

Basil No no. The other way round.

Manuel Ah! (*To the Halls*) Please.

They look at him. He indicates they should change places.

Colonel What?

Manuel Please to change.

Basil No, no, the <u>plates</u>!

Manuel Que?

Basil The plates! <u>Change</u> the plates!

Manuel ... Oh, <u>dirty</u>! I change.

He picks the plates up and makes for the kitchen. Basil intercepts him.

Basil No, no, come here, come here. Look ...

He takes the plates from Manuel, and demonstrates.

Manuel takes them with crossed arms. uncrosses them, and puts them down again exactly as before. Basil pulls Manuel away from the table and whispers to him. The Halls change their plates round themselves. Manuel returns from his briefing, and changes them back. He beams at the Halls. Basil comes up, bows, smiles and sees the plates.

Basil Sorry about this, he's from Barcelona.

He takes Manuel's arm and leads him away. The Halls exchange their plates a second time.

Basil (*to Manuel*) I don't know what he sees in you.

Basil returns to the Halls and, with an air of finality, switches their plates.

Basil Sorry about that.

He retires a pace or two. The Halls look at each other. Then, without a word they get up.

Basil jumps.

Mrs. Hall (*pointedly*) Do you think we could have a drink, dear?

Colonel Could we see the wine list, Fawlty?

Basil Certainly, Colonel.

Basil hurries to the sideboard, passing Twitchen. Twitchen is removing a long black hair from his mouth. He peers into his mousse suspiciously. Basil comes to the table on the way back with the wine list.

Basil Everything all right?

Mr. Twitchen (*doubtfully*) Er, yes . . .

Basil leans forward to address Mrs. Twitchen.

Basil Mrs. Twitchen?

Mr. Twitchen catches a glimpse of Basil's scalp. He stares at it.

Mrs. Twitchen Yes, yes everthing's fine thank you, Mr. Fawlty.

Basil Oh good.

Basil moves off . Twitchen nudges his wife and whispers urgently.

Mr. Twitchen He's got it in his hair !

Mrs. Twitchen What ?

Basil arrives back at the Halls' table. Mrs. Hall is just about to taste her first mouthful. Colonel Hall has just done so.

Mrs. Hall How is it, dear ?

Colonel Rather good, surprisingly.

She takes a mouthful.

Basil There's the list, Colonel.

Colonel Thank you.

Mrs. Hall lets out a shrill cry.

Mrs. Hall Ugh !

Basil freezes.

Colonel What's the matter, Petal ?

Mrs. Hall Ugggh !

Basil (*cheerfully*) Everything all right ?

Mrs. Hall (*grimacing unprecedentedly*) I think I'm going to be ill.

Basil It's an unusual taste, isn't it?

Mrs. Hall It hasn't been cooked, you ignoramus!

Colonel Look! What are you trying to do to us Fawlty? (*To Mrs. Hall*) Do you mean that's <u>raw</u>?

Basil Would you prefer it cooked?

Colonel Of course she'd prefer it cooked!!

Basil Certainly.

He whisks the plate away.

Basil I'll get you a cooked one, which will be even nicer.

In the kitchen

Sybil is working at the vegetables with Polly. Manuel is with Kurt who is propped up against the wall. Basil rushes in with the plate.

Basil It's raw! This mullet is raw! What do we do to it?

They all look blankly at him. He runs over to Kurt, and kneels in front of him.

Basil Kurt! Kurt, now listen . . . <u>what</u> <u>do</u> <u>we</u> <u>do</u> <u>with</u> <u>this</u>?

Kurt groans quietly.

Basil Do we <u>grill</u> it? . . .

Kurt opens up his eyes, stares at the mullet and groans.

Basil Look, if we grill this . . . just go 'uh-huh'

Kurt makes the slightest head-shaking movement.

Basil All right! Do we <u>fry</u> it?
Just go 'uh-huh'.

Kurt rolls his eyes and throws up over the plate.

Basil appraises Mrs. Hall's starter.

Basil . . . Going well, isn't it?

Sybil steps forward briskly, taking over.

> **Sybil** Basil, will you just get out. I will deal with the fish. Just go and get the duck.

She ushers him out.

> **Basil** (*not unwillingly*) Right. Right. Oh!! Wine!

> **Sybil** What?

> **Basil** The Colonel wants some wine. I'll just . . .

*He takes a pace towards the dining room
and then checks himself.*

> **Basil** No, you go, Polly.
> He won't hit a woman.

Basil turns and dashes for the front door.

In the dining room

*Polly enters, and approaches the Colonel,
who is peering closely at his mousse.*

> **Polly** (*slightly tentatively*) Have you . . . have you chosen yet, Colonel?

> **Colonel** Mmm?

> **Polly** Have you chosen your wine?

> **Colonel** (*not looking up*) Chablis . . .

*Polly picks up the wine list and turns
away.*

> **Colonel** Waitress!

> **Polly** . . . Yes?

> **Colonel** (*heavily*) There's a hair in my mousse.

Polly . . . Well, don't talk too loud or everyone will want one.

She smiles nervously. A pause. The Colonel roars.

Colonel . . . What!!!!

Polly Sorry.

She snatches the mousse away and hurries off with it. The Colonel twitches.

In the forecourt

Basil runs round the car and jumps in. He starts it, at the second attempt, and backs down the drive.

In the dining room

Manuel is inserting a corkscrew in the Chablis, watched by the Halls. Polly hastens in with another portion of mousse and puts it down in front of the Colonel.

Polly (*charmingly*) I'm sorry about that. (*To Mrs. Hall*) The mullet's on its way.

In the streets of Torquay

Basil is driving along, muttering at other motorists.

Basil Come on, come on! Oh, <u>thank</u> you, thank you <u>so</u> much.

He draws up outside André's restaurant, jumps out of the car, and races inside.

In André's kitchen

There is culinary activity. André is directing operations. Basil hurries in. André has the duck ready on a serving dish. He shows it to Basil, puts a cover over it and hands it to him, along with the sauces.

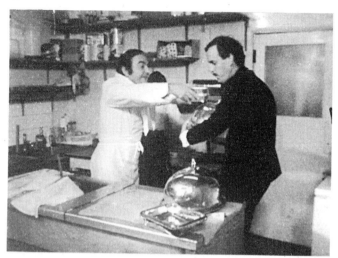

In the street outside

Basil jumps in the car, and tries to start it. It won't.

> **Basil** Come on! Come on!!

In the dining room

Manuel is standing ,waiting attentively as the Colonel tastes his new wine. He nods and twitches.

> **Manuel** No good?

> **Colonel** What? No, it's fine.

Manuel pours wine for Mrs. Hall, and then fills up the Colonel's glass. The Colonel sips from it. Manuel tops it up again the moment he takes it from his lips. The Colonel jumps, spilling some. Manuel tops it up again.

In the forecourt

Basil drives in through the gates. Polly, waiting at the top of the steps, sees the car and runs inside the hotel. Basil leaps out of the car with the duck, runs up the steps and into the lobby.

In the kitchen

*Polly has the vegetables ready as Basil
runs in.*

Basil Here we are! Sybil, the sauces!

*Sybil takes the box and starts putting the
sauces in appropriate dishes. Basil takes
a quick peek at the duck. It looks fine.*

Basil I'll carve it on the trolley. <u>Well</u> <u>done</u>, everybody!! Get the
trolley, Manuel.

Manuel. Si.

*Manuel runs through the swing doors to
the dining room, with Basil just behind him.
Sybil waves a sauce dish at Basil. She
hasn't quite finished.*

Sybil Basil!!

*Basil stops and turns. The doors swing back
and knock the duck out of Basil's hands.*

Basil Oh my God!

Basil Look what you've done you stupid great tart!!!

Polly suddenly darts forward.

Polly Wait a moment! It's all right . . .

Basil is still dazed.

Basil . . . What?!

Polly I think it's all <u>right</u>!

Basil drops to his knees and peers at it. It is intact!

Basil . . . Yes!!

Joyfully he reaches for it. The swing door opens and catches him a fearful blow on the head.

Manuel enters, treads in the duck and walks several paces with it on his foot. Basil howls, springs at Manuel and tries to get the shoe out of the duck.

The duck comes off. But the poor thing is terribly injured.

Basil Look ! Look at it !

Sybil Can I help ?

Basil Yes ! Go and kill yourself. No ! ! ! Call <u>André</u> ! Tell him we need another one.

He throws the duck at Kurt.

Basil Go and entertain them!!

Polly What?

Basil Play them some music or something.

In the lobby

Sybil Oh, André, it's Sybil Fawlty...
Well, I'm afraid it got trodden on...

In the forecourt

In the dining room

In the streets of Torquay

In André's kitchen

André is looking into an oven. When Basil bursts in, he whips a duck out of the oven and on to another serving tray, slipping a cover over it. Basil is about to pick it up when André distracts him by offering him some fresh sauces. As he is looking away, a waiter puts a similar tray and cover next to the duck. Basil declines the sauces, turns and picks up the wrong one.
He hurries out, thanking André profusely.

In the street outside

Basil vaults into the car, and presses the starter. It fires plaintively.

Basil I'll get you for this! Come <u>on</u>!

In the dining room

Manuel has finished his song.

A pause.

Polly (*singing*) I'm just a girl who can't say 'No'.

In the streets of Torquay

Basil turns into a narrow road. It is blocked by a parked van. Basil curses, hits his horn, waits, gives up, reverses back and stalls. He tries to start the car again. This time it refuses completely. Basil becomes more frantic.

Basil Start will you!? Start, you bastard!! Oh my God! You stupid, vicious, bastard I'm warning you if you don't start . . .

He screams with rage.

Basil I'm going to count up to three.

He presses the starter. Without success.

Basil One . . . two . . . <u>three</u>!! Right! That's it!

Basil jumps out of the car and addresses it.

Basil I'm going to give you a piece of my mind. I've never liked you, you son-of-a-bitch, you've never run right, you've had it in for me right from the beginning haven't you? Well, you've had this coming to you! I'm going to give you a damn good thrashing.

Basil disappears.

Back in the dining room

Polly ends her song.

Polly . . . can't . . . say . . . 'No'.

Colonel (*loudly*) Any sign of the duck?

Polly Er . . . it's just coming.

In the forecourt

In the dining room

Sybil is the next on.

Sybil So Uncle Ted walks in with this crate of brown ale, ha, ha, ha, . . . and Mother says 'Oh Ted look who's here'. And Ted says 'Hallo, dear! What are you . . .'

In the kitchen

Basil comes flying in, slides to a halt, looks around, and sees Polly who has the vegetables at the ready.

Basil O.K. Polly ?!

Polly O.K. !

Basil Don't forget the sauces !

Polly Got them !

In the dining room

Basil enters in triumph. He places the duck on the trolly and ceremoniously wheels it forward.

Basil Ladies and gentlemen!!

Basil (*brightly*) Well, who's for trifle?

Colonel (*dangerously*) What about
the duck, Fawlty?

Basil . . . Duck's off, sorry.

FAWLTY TOWERS
PRODUCTION TEAM

Producer	**John Howard Davies**
Producer's Assistant	**Angela Sharp**
Designer	**Peter Kindred**
Sound	**John Howell**
Lighting	**Geoff Shaw**
	Ron Koplick
Production Assistant	**Tony Guyan**
Make-up	**Jean Speak**
Costumes	**Mary Woods**
Tape Editors	**Pete Dunkley**
	Chris Booth
	Derek Orman
Film Editor	**Bob Rymer**
Film Cameraman	**Stan Speel**
Music	**Dennis Wilson**
Vision Mixer	**Bill Morton**